Natural Remedies for Backyard Chickens: A comprehensive Guide to Health and wellness

Glenda Jones

contents

INTRODUCTION

There are several reasons why people choose to use natural remedies on chickens:

1. Minimize Chemical Exposure: Natural remedies offer an alternative to conventional treatments that may involve the use of synthetic chemicals. Some chicken keepers prefer natural remedies to reduce chemical exposure in their flock and promote a more holistic approach to chicken health.

2. Sustainable and Organic Practices: Natural remedies align with the principles of sustainable and organic practices. By using natural remedies, chicken keepers can avoid or reduce reliance on pharmaceuticals and chemicals, opting for more environmentally friendly options.

3. Preventive Care: Natural remedies are often used as part of a preventive care approach. By incorporating herbs,

supplements, and other natural remedies for a chicken's routine, it's believed that overall health and immunity can be supported, potentially reducing the risk of certain ailments.

4. Traditional Knowledge and Folk Wisdom: Natural remedies for chickens have been passed down through generations of poultry keepers. Many of these remedies are based on traditional knowledge and folk wisdom that has been used for years to maintain the health and well-being of chickens.

5. Limited Access to Veterinary Care: In some cases, chicken keepers may have limited access to veterinary care or prefer to try natural remedies as a first-line approach before seeking professional help. Natural remedies can be more accessible and affordable, especially for backyard chicken enthusiasts who may not have easy access to poultry veterinarians.

6. Personal Beliefs and Lifestyle Choices: Some people choose to use natural remedies on chickens based on their personal beliefs, values, or lifestyle choices. This can include a preference for natural or holistic approaches to animal care and a desire to minimize the use of synthetic substances

This book is approached by topic in alphabetical order.

ALTERNATIVE DIETS

When it comes to raising backyard chickens, their diet plays a crucial role in their overall health, egg production, and well-being. While traditional chicken feed is a staple, there's a growing interest in exploring alternative diets that offer nutritional diversity and environmental benefits. In this blog post, we'll delve into some alternative diets for chickens that can contribute to their overall health and provide you with the satisfaction of knowing exactly what your feathered friends are consuming.

Kitchen Scraps and Leftovers:

One of the simplest ways to supplement your chickens' diet is by providing them with kitchen scraps and leftovers. Chickens are omnivores and can thrive on a variety of foods, including fruit and vegetable scraps, rice, pasta, and bread. However, it's essential to avoid giving them anything spoiled, moldy, or toxic, as well as too much of any one type of food. Adding kitchen scraps not only reduces waste but also enhances their diet with additional nutrients.

Grains and Seeds:

Grains and seeds are another excellent addition to your chickens' diet. Options like oats, barley, and sunflower seeds can provide them with essential carbohydrates and healthy fats. These grains can be scattered in their coop or run, encouraging natural foraging behaviors and mental stimulation.

Insects and Worms:

Chickens are natural foragers and love to hunt for insects and worms. Providing them with access to grassy areas can help them find bugs and worms that are rich in protein and other nutrients. Additionally, mealworms, crickets, and black soldier fly larvae are popular treats that can be purchased as supplements to their diet.

Fresh Greens and Herbs:

Introducing fresh greens and herbs into your chickens' diet not only adds variety but also contributes essential vitamins and minerals. Offer them treats like lettuce, kale, spinach, and herbs like parsley and basil. These greens can be chopped or hung in their coop to encourage pecking and foraging.

Grubs and Fish:

Introducing protein-rich foods like grubs and fish can offer a natural boost to your chickens' diet. Black soldier fly larvae, commonly known as grubs, are a high-protein snack that can be a valuable addition. Additionally, small fish like minnows can be provided occasionally, as they offer omega-3 fatty acids that are beneficial for egg quality.

While traditional chicken feed remains a reliable option, exploring alternative diets for your backyard chickens can enhance their nutritional intake, support their overall health, and promote natural foraging behaviors. Keep in mind that any dietary changes should be introduced gradually and monitored to ensure your chickens are thriving. By incorporating a mix of kitchen scraps, grains, seeds, insects, worms, greens, and other protein-rich treats, you're offering your feathered companions a well-rounded and enjoyable diet that contributes to their happiness and vitality.

Apple Cider Vinegar (ACV)

Apple cider vinegar (ACV) is a type of vinegar made from fermented apple juice. It has gained popularity in recent years for its potential health benefits and various household uses. Here are some common uses and benefits of apple cider vinegar:

1. **Antimicrobial Properties:** ACV has antimicrobial properties, thanks to its acetic acid content. It may help inhibit the growth of certain bacteria and fungi. Some people use it as a natural household cleaner or as a skin toner to help fight acne-causing bacteria.

2. **Skin and Hair Care:** ACV is sometimes used as a natural remedy for skin and hair conditions. It may help balance the pH of the skin, soothe irritation, and clarify the scalp.

However, it's important to dilute it properly and perform a patch test before using it on the skin or hair.

3. **Cleaning and Household Uses:** ACV can be an effective natural cleaning agent due to its acidic nature. It can be used to clean surfaces, remove stains, neutralize odors, and act as a natural fabric softener.

When using ACV, it's important to remember the following:

• Dilute ACV before using it on the skin or hair to avoid irritation.

If consumed, it's best to dilute ACV in water or use it as an ingredient in recipes rather than consuming it undiluted. Antimicrobial refers to substances or treatments that have the ability to kill or inhibit the growth of microorganisms, including bacteria, viruses, fungi, and protozoa. Unlike antibacterial, which specifically targets bacteria, antimicrobial encompasses a broader spectrum of microorganisms.

Here are some examples of antimicrobial substances and practices:

1. **Antimicrobial Agents in Cleaning Products:** Many cleaning products, such as surface cleaners and disinfectants, contain antimicrobial ingredients. These substances help kill or reduce the growth of various microorganisms on surfaces.

2. **Antimicrobial Hand Sanitizers:** Hand sanitizers that are labeled as antimicrobial are designed to kill a broad range of microorganisms on the skin, including bacteria and viruses. They often contain alcohol or other active ingredients.

3. **Antimicrobial Treatments for Surfaces:** Some products are specifically formulated to provide antimicrobial protection for surfaces, such as countertops, cutting boards, and medical equipment. These treatments help inhibit the growth of bacteria, viruses, and other pathogens.

4. **Antimicrobial Agents in Personal Care Products:** Certain personal care products, such as deodorants, body washes, and toothpaste, may contain antimicrobial ingredients. These substances help prevent the growth of bacteria or fungi that can cause odors or oral health issues.

5. **Antimicrobial Fabrics:** Some textiles and materials are treated with antimicrobial agents to inhibit the growth of microorganisms. These fabrics are commonly used in healthcare settings, sports apparel, and other applications where microbial control is desired.

6. **Antimicrobial Peptides:** Antimicrobial peptides are naturally occurring compounds that can be found in organisms, including humans. These peptides have antimicrobial properties and help protect against microbial infections.

7. **Antimicrobial Preservatives:** Certain food and cosmetic products contain antimicrobial preservatives to prevent the growth of microorganisms and extend shelf life. Common antimicrobial preservatives include parabens, benzalkonium chloride, and sorbic acid.

It's important to note that the use of antimicrobial substances should be done responsibly and in accordance with product instructions. Overuse or misuse of antimicrobial agents can contribute to the development of resistance among microorganisms, making them less susceptible to treatment. Proper hygiene practices, regular cleaning, and maintaining a balanced and healthy environment are also essential for controlling the spread of microorganisms

Avian Influenza

A vian influenza, commonly known as bird flu, is a highly contagious viral disease that can have devastating effects on poultry
populations. Recognizing the symptoms, implementing effective prevention measures, and knowing how to manage outbreaks are crucial
aspects of safeguarding your flock's health. In this chapter, we will
delve into the complexities of avian influenza, from its causes and
symptoms to strategies for prevention and management.

Understanding Avian Influenza:

Avian influenza is caused by various strains of influenza viruses,
primarily affecting birds. It can lead to a range of symptoms, including
severe respiratory distress, decreased egg production, and high mortality rates in affected chickens. The disease can spread rapidly, posing
significant risks to poultry populations.

Common Signs of Avian Influenza:

1. **Respiratory Symptoms:**

   ○ Chickens may exhibit signs such as coughing, sneezing,
     nasal discharge, and labored breathing.

2. **Reduced Egg Production:**

- Infected hens may experience a sharp decline in egg-laying productivity or even a complete cessation of egg production.

3. **Swelling and Discoloration of Combs and Wattles:**

- These areas may become dark, swollen, and discolored due to reduced blood flow.

4. **Lethargy and Weakness:**

- Chickens suffering from avian influenza often display signs of lethargy, weakness, and reluctance to move.

5. **Digestive Symptoms:**

- Diarrhea and digestive disturbances may be observed in some cases.

6. **Neurological Signs (in severe cases):**

- These may include tremors, lack of coordination, and paralysis.

Preventing Avian Influenza:

1. **Biosecurity Measures:**

- Implement strict biosecurity protocols to prevent the introduction and spread of avian influenza. This includes limiting access to the coop, quarantining new birds, and regularly disinfecting equipment.

2. Isolation and Quarantine:

- Immediately isolate any birds showing symptoms of avian influenza to prevent the spread of the virus.

3. Vaccination (where applicable):

- In some regions, vaccination against specific strains of avian influenza may be recommended. Consult with a veterinarian for guidance.

4. Restricted Access to Wild Birds:

- Limit exposure of your flock to wild birds, which can be carriers of avian influenza.

Managing Avian Influenza Outbreaks:

1. Seek Professional Guidance:

- In the event of an outbreak, consult with a veterinarian for a comprehensive management plan.

2. Cull Infected Birds (if necessary):

- In severe cases, euthanasia and proper disposal of infected birds may be required to prevent further spread.

3. Thorough Cleaning and Disinfection:

- Clean and disinfect the coop, equipment, and surrounding areas to eliminate any traces of the virus.

Avian influenza is a serious threat to poultry health, but with vigilance, proper biosecurity measures, and professional guidance, its impact can be minimized. Regular monitoring, strict adherence to biosecurity protocols, and swift action in the event of an outbreak are crucial in safeguarding your flock against this viral disease. By implementing these measures, you can promote the well-being and longevity of your chickens.

AVIAN (FOWL) POX

To determine if your chicken has avian pox, you need to look for specific symptoms and observe their behavior. Here are some signs that may indicate avian pox in chickens:

1. **Lesions:** Avian pox is characterized by the presence of raised, wart-like lesions on the chicken's skin, particularly on the unfathered areas of the head, face, comb, wattles, legs, and feet. The lesions can vary in size and color, appearing as grayish or yellowish bumps or scabs. In wet pox cases, lesions may also be present in the mouth, throat, trachea, and cloaca.

2. **Respiratory Symptoms:** In cases of wet pox, chickens may exhibit respiratory symptoms, such as sneezing, coughing, wheezing, or difficulty breathing. These symptoms are typically associated with lesions in the respiratory tract.

3. **Swollen Eyes:** Avian pox lesions near or on the eyes can cause swelling, redness, or discharge. Affected chickens may have difficulty opening their eyes fully or may exhibit signs of eye irritation.

4. **Reduced Appetite and Weight Loss:** Chickens with avian pox may show a decreased appetite, resulting in weight loss and lethargy. They may also exhibit a decrease in overall activity levels.

5. **Decreased Egg Production:** The disease can impact egg production in affected hens, leading to a reduction in the number of eggs laid or a temporary halt in egg production.

6. **Behavioral Changes:** Infected chickens may appear listless, depressed, or withdrawn. They may isolate themselves from the flock or exhibit reduced interaction with other birds.

It's important to note that the symptoms mentioned above can also be associated with other health issues in chickens. Therefore, a definitive diagnosis of avian pox should be confirmed by a veterinarian through clinical examination, laboratory testing, or by observing the characteristic lesions. If you suspect avian pox in your chicken, it is recommended to isolate the affected bird from the rest of the flock to prevent the spread of the virus. Contact a veterinarian for proper diagnosis, treatment options, and guidance on managing the disease within your flock

Beak Trimming

T rimming a chicken's beak is typically done for specific reasons, such as managing overgrown beaks or addressing certain behavioral issues. However, it is generally recommended to have the beak trimming procedure performed by a qualified professional, such as a veterinarian or an experienced poultry handler, as it requires proper knowledge and equipment to minimize potential harm to the bird. Beak trimming is not a routine procedure and should only be considered when necessary.

Here are some general guidelines on the process:

1. **Seek Professional Help:** Consult with a veterinarian or an experienced poultry handler who can assess the situation and determine if beak trimming is necessary. They can also guide you through the process or perform it for you.

2. **Anesthetize the Chicken (if required):** In some cases, beak trimming may require anesthetizing the chicken to minimize stress and discomfort. This should only be done by a professional who can administer and monitor the anesthesia safely.

3. **Choose the Right Equipment:** Beak trimming should be done using specialized tools designed for the purpose. These tools may include a beak trimmer or a hot blade specifically designed for poultry beak trimming.

4. **Proper Technique:** The exact technique used for beak trimming can vary depending on the specific situation and the type of beak trimmer being used.

Generally, the goal is to carefully remove a small portion of the beak's edge to achieve the desired length while avoiding injury to the sensitive tissue and blood vessels inside the beak.

5. **Address Bleeding and Provide Post-Procedure Care:** In some cases, there may be minor bleeding after beak trimming. Applying a mild styptic powder or cornstarch to the trimmed area can help stop the bleeding. It is important to monitor the chicken for any signs of complications and provide appropriate post-procedure care as advised by the professional.

Remember, beak trimming should only be done when

necessary and with the guidance of a professional. It is important to prioritize the welfare of the chicken and minimize any potential stress or harm during the procedure

BLOOD OR MEAT SPOTS IN EGGS

Discovering blood spots on the outside of a chicken egg can be disconcerting for backyard chicken keepers. However, while it might look alarming, these blood spots are actually quite common and typically pose no harm to consumers. In this blog post, we'll delve into the reasons behind blood spots on chicken eggs, why they occur, and whether you should be concerned.

Why Do Blood Spots Occur?

Blood spots, also known as "meat spots," can occasionally appear on the outside of chicken eggs. These spots are tiny and usually reddish-brown in color. They are the result of a ruptured blood vessel in the hen's reproductive system during egg formation. While blood spots can be more noticeable on the eggshell, they can also be present on the egg's interior.

Causes of Blood Spots:

Hormonal Fluctuations: The process of egg formation involves hormonal changes in the hen's reproductive system. Sometimes, a small blood vessel might break during this process, leading to a blood spot.

Age of the Hen: Young hens that are just beginning to lay eggs are more prone to blood spots. As hens mature, the likelihood of blood spots occurring decreases.

Genetics: Certain breeds or individual hens might be more predisposed to developing blood spots due to their genetics.

Diet and Stress: An imbalanced diet or stressful conditions can impact egg production and quality, potentially leading to blood spots.

Vitamin Deficiencies: Deficiencies in certain vitamins, particularly vitamin K, can increase the likelihood of blood spots.

Is It Safe to Consume Eggs with Blood Spots?

Yes, eggs with small blood spots are safe to eat. Blood spots are not indicative of a fertilized egg or any health risk. They are harmless and do not affect the taste, nutritional value, or quality of the egg. If the sight of a blood spot bothers you, you can simply remove it before cooking.

Preventing Blood Spots:

While blood spots are generally unavoidable and occur naturally, there are a few steps you can take to minimize their occurrence:

Provide a Balanced Diet: Ensure your hens receive a well-balanced diet that includes all essential nutrients, especially vitamin K.

Reduce Stress: A calm and stress-free environment for your chickens can contribute to overall egg quality.

Regular Health Checks: Regularly monitor your chickens' health and ensure they are not experiencing any underlying health issues.

Finding a blood spot on the outside of a chicken egg might be surprising, but it's a normal occurrence in egg production. Understanding the causes and knowing that these spots are harmless can ease any concerns. When collecting eggs, simply brush off or remove any blood spots before cooking and enjoy your fresh and nutritious homegrown eggs without worry.

Boredom Busters

1. **Hanging Treats:** Suspend fruits or vegetables from the coop ceiling for a fun and challenging feeding activity.

2. **Chicken-Safe Herbs:** Plant a small herb garden near the coop. Chickens enjoy pecking at and exploring herbs like mint, parsley, and basil.

3. **Dust Bath Area:** Provide a designated area with dry dirt and sand for your chickens to indulge in their natural dust bathing behavior.

4. **Mirror or Reflective Surfaces:** Install a mirror or reflective object in the coop for visual stimulation.

5. **Scatter Grains:** Scatter small portions of grains or seeds in the coop to encourage foraging behavior.

6. **Treat Balls or Feeders:** Use treat-dispensing balls or toys to

make them work for their treats.

7. **Swinging Perch:** Install a swinging perch in the coop for a playful and interactive experience.

8. **Small Flock Rivalry:** Introduce a temporary partition to create two smaller flocks. This encourages social interaction and helps break the monotony.

9. **Garden Greens:** Allow chickens to forage in a controlled garden area with edible plants like clover, dandelions, and lettuce.

10. **Cabbage Pinata:** Hang a whole cabbage from the coop ceiling and let your chickens peck at it for a tasty treat.

11. **Corn-on-the-Cob Holder:** Attach corn-on-the-cob holders to the coop walls for a fun pecking activity.

12. **Wooden Spools:** Attach wooden spools to a wire for chickens to play with and roll around.

13. **Puzzle Feeders:** Invest in puzzle feeders designed for chickens, where they must figure out how to access the treats inside.

14. **Treat Stations:** Create designated treat stations with different types of treats or feed scattered on a flat surface.

15. **Logs or Branches:** Place logs or branches in the coop for chickens to explore and perch on.

16. **Hang Greens:** Tie bunches of leafy greens like kale or Swiss chard from the coop ceiling.

17. **Plastic Balls with Holes:** Fill plastic balls with holes with treats or grains for your chickens to roll around and extract treats from.

18. **Mini Obstacle Course:** Create a mini obstacle course with small ramps, tunnels, and platforms for chickens to navigate.

19. **Pecking Boards:** Attach boards with small, easily peckable treats like mealworms or sunflower seeds.

20. **Sprouted Grains:** Sprout grains like wheat or barley and scatter them in the coop for a nutritious snack.

21. **Frozen Treats:** Freeze fruits, vegetables, or mealworms in ice cubes for a refreshing and engaging activity.

22. **Pine Cone Treats:** Roll pine cones in peanut butter and then in seeds for a natural and tasty boredom buster.

23. **Floating Treats:** Place treats or fruits in a shallow dish of water for a fun floating treasure hunt.

24. **Digital Entertainment:** Set up a tablet with a video of bugs or worms moving around to provide visual stimulation.

25. **Chicken-Safe Toys:** Introduce toys designed for chickens, such as hanging feeders with movable parts or small bales of hay with hidden treats.

Remember to regularly rotate and switch out the activities to keep things fresh and engaging for your feathered friends. Providing mental and physical stimulation is essential for the well-being of your chickens!

Bronchitis

I nfectious Bronchitis (IB) is a highly contagious respiratory disease caused by a coronavirus that affects chickens worldwide. Recognizing the symptoms, and implementing appropriate natural remedies, can be crucial in managing and alleviating the discomfort associated with this ailment. In this chapter, we will explore various natural approaches to support your flock during an Infectious Bronchitis outbreak.

Understanding Infectious Bronchitis:

Infectious Bronchitis is caused by a coronavirus that primarily targets the respiratory system of chickens. It leads to respiratory distress, coughing, sneezing, and nasal discharge. Young chickens and those with weakened immune systems are particularly susceptible.

Natural Remedies for Infectious Bronchitis:

1. **Herbal Infusions:**

   ○ **Thyme and Oregano:** These herbs have natural antibacterial and antiviral properties. Add dried thyme or oregano to their drinking water or provide fresh sprigs in their coop.

- Echinacea: Boosts the immune system and aids in recovery. Infuse dried echinacea into their drinking water.

2. **Vitamin-Rich Foods:**

- **Leafy Greens:** Provide nutrient-rich greens like kale, spinach, and Swiss chard to support overall health and boost immunity.

- **Fruits:** Offer vitamin C-rich fruits like oranges, berries, and kiwi to strengthen the immune system.

3. **Garlic and Ginger:**

- **Garlic:** Known for its natural antibiotic properties, garlic can be added to their feed or water. Crush a clove and mix it with their food.

- **Ginger:** Acts as an anti-inflammatory and immune-boosting agent. Grate fresh ginger and mix it with their food.

4. **Honey and Lemon:**

- **Honey:** Contains natural antibacterial properties and soothes the throat. Mix with warm water and offer it as a drink.

- **Lemon:** Rich in vitamin C, lemon can help boost the immune system. Add a few drops of lemon juice to their water.

5. Essential Oils:

- **Eucalyptus and Peppermint:** These oils have respiratory benefits. Diffuse a small amount in the coop or dilute them for a topical application.

- **Tea Tree Oil:** Known for its antiviral properties, use a small amount in a diffuser to help purify the air.

6. Probiotics and Fermented Foods:

- **Yogurt or Kefir:** Contains beneficial bacteria that support a healthy gut and boost the immune system.

- **Fermented Vegetables:** Provide probiotics and enhance digestive health. Offer small amounts of fermented vegetables like sauerkraut.

7. Steam Therapy:

- Create a warm, humid environment in the coop to help alleviate respiratory distress. Use a humidifier or provide a warm water vapor bath.

8. Isolation and Quarantine:

- Immediately isolate affected birds to prevent the spread of the virus to the rest of the flock.

While natural remedies can help support chickens suffering from Infectious Bronchitis, it's essential to consult with a veterinarian for severe cases or if symptoms persist. Combining natural remedies with good husbandry practices, such as clean living conditions and a balanced diet, will contribute to the overall health and well-being of your flock during this challenging time.

BUMBLEFOOT

B umblefoot, also known as pododermatitis, is a common
condition in chickens characterized by inflammation and
infection in the foot. It can be caused by various factors, such
as injury, rough surfaces, or bacterial infections. While I can
provide some general remedies for bumblefoot, it's
important to note that veterinary advice should always be
sought for proper diagnosis and treatment.

Here are some general remedies and steps you can take to
help treat bumblefoot in chickens:

1. **Isolate the affected chicken:** Separate the chicken from
the flock to prevent further injury or spreading of infection.

2. **Clean the affected foot**: Gently clean the affected foot
with mild antiseptic solution or warm saline water. This will

help remove dirt and bacteria. Be careful not to cause further damage or pain to the chicken.

3. **Soak the foot:** Prepare a warm Epsom salt soak and gently immerse the chicken's foot in it for about 15-20 minutes. This can help soften the scab and reduce swelling. Make sure to dry the foot thoroughly afterward.

4. **Remove the scab or core:** Once the foot has been soaked, you may try to remove the scab or core of the bumblefoot using sterile instruments. This should be done carefully to avoid causing pain or bleeding. If you're unsure or uncomfortable doing this, it's best to consult a veterinarian.

5. **Apply antibiotic ointment:** After removing the scab, apply a topical antibiotic ointment, such as a triple antibiotic ointment, to the affected area. This can help prevent or treat any bacterial infection. Make sure to follow the instructions provided and apply the ointment as directed.

6. **Bandage the foot:** To protect the foot from further injury and to keep it clean, you can bandage it using a non-stick pad and self-adhesive bandage wrap. Be cautious not to wrap it too tightly, as it can restrict circulation. Change the bandage regularly to prevent infection.

7. **Provide pain relief and supportive care:** If your chicken is experiencing pain or discomfort, you can offer pain relief by providing access to clean water, a balanced diet, and a

calm, stress-free environment. Ensure the chicken has a clean and comfortable place to rest.

8. **Monitor and maintain hygiene:** Regularly check the foot for any signs of improvement or worsening. Keep the coop and bedding clean to minimize bacterial contamination and prevent reinfection.

Remember, bumblefoot can vary in severity, and in some cases, surgical intervention may be necessary to completely remove the infection. It's crucial to consult a veterinarian experienced in avian care for an accurate diagnosis and appropriate treatment plan for your chicken's bumblefoot

COCCIDIOS

C occidiosis is a common and potentially devastating parasitic disease that affects chickens worldwide. Caused by a protozoa called coccidia, this ailment primarily targets the intestinal tract, leading to a range of symptoms including diarrhea, weight loss, and reduced egg production. In this comprehensive guide, we will delve into the intricacies of coccidiosis, from its causes and symptoms to effective management strategies.

Understanding Coccidiosis:

Coccidiosis is caused by several species of the protozoan parasite coccidia. These parasites thrive in warm, humid environments and are commonly found in the soil and environment where chickens are raised. When ingested, coccidia multiply within the intestinal lining, causing damage and leading to a range of clinical signs.

Common Signs of Coccidiosis:

1. **Diarrhea:** One of the most prominent and early signs of coccidiosis is watery or bloody diarrhea.

2. **Weight Loss:** Chickens affected by coccidiosis may experi-

ence a significant loss of body weight.

3. **Decreased Egg Production:** Hens may exhibit a sharp decline in egg-laying productivity.

4. **Lethargy and Weakness:** Infected chickens often display signs of lethargy, weakness, and reluctance to move.

5. **Poor Appetite:** A decrease in appetite and reluctance to eat may be observed.

6. **Preening and Ruffled Feathers:** Chickens suffering from coccidiosis may spend more time preening and have ruffled feathers.

7. **Dehydration:** Severe cases of coccidiosis can lead to dehydration, which further exacerbates the condition.

Managing Coccidiosis:

1. **Isolation and Quarantine:**

   o Immediately isolate infected birds to prevent the spread of coccidia to the rest of the flock.

2. **Sanitation and Hygiene:**

   o Maintain clean and dry living conditions, regularly removing feces and contaminated bedding.

3. **Proper Ventilation:**

   o Ensure adequate airflow within the coop to reduce humidity and create an environment less conducive to coccidia.

4. Balanced Diet:

○ Provide a balanced and nutritionally complete diet to support the overall health and immune function of the chickens.

5. Hydration:

○ Ensure access to clean, fresh water at all times to prevent dehydration.

6. Coccidiostats and Natural Remedies:

○ Consult with a veterinarian for appropriate coccidiostat medications or inquire about natural remedies like oregano oil or apple cider vinegar.

7. Vaccination:

○ In some cases, vaccination against specific strains of coccidia may be recommended. Consult with a veterinarian for guidance.

Coccidiosis is a serious threat to poultry health, but with proper understanding and management strategies, its impact can be minimized. Regular monitoring, maintaining cleanliness, and seeking professional advice when needed are vital steps in safeguarding your flock against this parasitic disease. By implementing these measures, you can promote the well-being and longevity of your chickens.

10 Common Diseases

The following are 10 common diseases that backyard chickens may experience:

1. **Marek's Disease:** Marek's disease is a highly contagious viral disease that affects chickens, causing tumors and neurological symptoms.

2. **Infectious Bronchitis:** Infectious bronchitis is a respiratory disease caused by a coronavirus, resulting in respiratory distress, coughing, and sneezing.

3. **Coccidiosis:** Coccidiosis is a parasitic disease caused by protozoa called coccidia, which affects the intestinal tract, leading to diarrhea, weight loss, and decreased egg production.

4. **Avian Influenza:** Avian influenza, or bird flu, is a viral

disease that can cause severe respiratory symptoms, decreased egg production, and high mortality rates in chickens.

5. **Newcastle Disease:** Newcastle disease is a viral infection that affects the respiratory, gastrointestinal, and nervous systems, leading to respiratory distress, neurological symptoms, and high mortality.

6. **Fowl Pox:** Fowl pox is a viral disease characterized by the formation of lesions on the skin, mouth, and respiratory tract, resulting in decreased appetite and decreased egg production.

7. **Salmonellosis:** Salmonellosis is a bacterial infection caused by Salmonella, which can cause diarrhea, lethargy, decreased appetite, and even death in severe cases.

8. **Ectoparasites:** External parasites such as mites, lice, and fleas can infest chickens, leading to irritation, feather loss, anemia, and overall poor health.

9. **Mycoplasma Gallisepticum:** Mycoplasma gallisepticum is a bacterial infection that causes respiratory symptoms, including coughing, sneezing, and nasal discharge.

10. **Egg-related issues:** Various egg-related problems can occur, including egg binding (difficulty laying eggs), egg peritonitis (infection of the abdominal cavity), or prolapsed oviduct (protrusion of the oviduct).

clean coop

C leaning a chicken coop is an important part of maintaining a healthy and sanitary environment for your chickens.

Here are the general steps to clean a chicken coop:

1. **Gather the necessary supplies:** Prepare the following supplies before starting the cleaning process:
• Protective gloves
• Face mask (if desired)
• Rake or shovel
• Broom or brush
• Bucket or wheelbarrow
• Scrub brush or stiff broom
• Mild detergent or poultry-safe disinfectant
• Hose or water source

2. **Prepare the coop:** Remove chickens from the coop and secure them in a safe area or separate run. Make sure they have access to food, water, and shelter during the cleaning process.

3. **Remove bedding and Debris:** Start by removing all bedding materials, such as straw, wood shavings, or hay. Use a rake or shovel to scoop out the soiled bedding, droppings, feathers, and any other debris from the coop floor.

4. **Dispose of waste:** Place the soiled bedding and debris into a bucket, wheelbarrow, or other suitable container for proper disposal. Consider composting the waste in a designated compost area if desired.

5. **Scrub the coop:** Use a scrub brush or stiff broom to scrub all surfaces inside the coop, including walls, floors, perches, nesting boxes, and any other surfaces that may have become soiled. Remove any stuck-on dirt or droppings.

6. **Rinse with water:** Once the scrubbing is complete, thoroughly rinse the coop using a hose or water source. Make sure to remove all detergent residue and dirt from the surfaces.

7. **Disinfect (optional):** If desired or necessary, you can use a mild detergent or poultry-safe disinfectant to further sanitize the coop. Follow the manufacturer's instructions for

dilution and application. Pay extra attention to areas that may harbor parasites or bacteria, such as nesting boxes and roosting areas.

8. **Allow the coop to dry:** After rinsing and disinfecting (if applicable), allow the coop to air dry completely. Ensure good ventilation to expedite the drying process and prevent moisture buildup.

9. **Replace bedding:** Once the coop is dry, spread a fresh layer of clean bedding material, such as straw, wood shavings, or pine shavings, on the coop floor and in nesting boxes.

10. **Return chickens to the coop**: Once the coop is clean and dry and the bedding is replaced, allow the chickens to return to their freshly cleaned home.

It's important to establish a regular cleaning schedule based on the size of your flock and the condition of the coop. Maintaining a clean coop will help prevent the buildup of parasites, bacteria, and unpleasant odors, ensuring a healthier and more comfortable environment for your chickens.

There are several poultry-safe disinfectants available on the market that are formulated specifically for use in poultry environments. When choosing a poultry-safe disinfectant, look for products that are labeled as safe for use around chickens and other poultry.

Here are a few examples of commonly used poultry-safe disinfectants:

1. **Quaternary Ammonium Compounds (Quats):** These are a group of disinfectants that are effective against a wide range of bacteria, viruses, and fungi. Some poultry-safe quats include Roccal®-D Plus, Virkon® S, and BioSentry® 904 Disinfectant.

2. **Chlorine-Based Disinfectants:** Chlorine-based disinfectants, such as bleach, can be used for poultry disinfection. It's important to dilute bleach properly according to the manufacturer's instructions and thoroughly rinse the treated surfaces afterward. Avoid direct contact of undiluted bleach with birds.

3. **Peroxygen Compounds:** Peroxygen-based disinfectants, like hydrogen peroxide, are considered safe for use in poultry facilities. They have antimicrobial properties and can help control pathogens. Follow the instructions on the product label for appropriate dilution and application.

4. **Iodine-Based Disinfectants:** Iodine-based disinfectants, such as Betadine®, can be used for poultry sanitation. They are effective against various pathogens and are generally safe when used according to instructions. Rinse surfaces thoroughly after application.

5. **Citric Acid-Based Disinfectants:** Citric acid-based

disinfectants, such as F10® SC Veterinary Disinfectant, are considered safe for use around poultry. They have antimicrobial properties and are effective against a range of pathogens

Remember to carefully read and follow the instructions provided by the manufacturer when using any disinfectant. This includes information on dilution ratios, contact time, and safety precautions. Additionally, always ensure proper ventilation when using any disinfectant to protect both you and your chickens. If you are uncertain about the safety of a specific disinfectant, consult with a veterinarian or poultry health professional for guidance.

Crop issues

Crop issues can occur when the crop, a pouch-like structure in the chicken's digestive system, becomes impacted or develops an infection. Symptoms may include a swollen, hard, or sour-smelling crop, regurgitation, weight loss, and decreased appetite

Deworming

Diatomaceous Earth

D iatomaceous earth (DE) is a naturally occurring, sedimentary rock made up of the fossilized remains of diatoms, which are tiny aquatic organisms. DE is commonly used for various purposes, including as a natural insecticide and pest control agent.

Here's some information about diatomaceous earth:

1. **Physical Properties:** Diatomaceous earth appears as a fine, powdery substance that feels abrasive to the touch. It is composed mostly of silica, along with traces of other minerals. DE can come in different grades, such as food grade and industrial grade, depending on its purity and intended use.

2. **Pest Control:** One of the primary uses of diatomaceous earth is for pest control, particularly against crawling insects.

The microscopic sharp edges of the diatomaceous earth particles can penetrate the exoskeleton of insects, causing them to dehydrate and die. DE is effective against pests like ants, cockroaches, fleas, bed bugs, and mites.

3. **Application:** Diatomaceous earth can be applied in various ways:

• **Indoor Use:** Sprinkle DE in areas where pests are likely to crawl, such as along baseboards, in cracks and crevices, and around entry points. It can also be applied to carpets, upholstery, and pet bedding to combat fleas.

• **Outdoor Use:** Apply DE around the perimeter of your home, garden, or coop to create a barrier against crawling insects. It can also be dusted onto plants to control pests.

• **Personal Protection:** Some people use food-grade diatomaceous earth as a natural insect repellent by dusting it onto their skin or clothing to deter pests like ticks.

4. **Safety Considerations:** When using diatomaceous earth, it's important to consider the following:

• **Choose Food-Grade DE:** If you plan to use diatomaceous earth around food, pets, or for personal use, make sure to use food-grade DE. Industrialgrade DE may contain

additional additives or
impurities that could be harmful.

• **Use Protective Gear:** To avoid inhaling the fine
particles of diatomaceous earth, it's advisable to wear
a mask, gloves, and protective eyewear during
application.

• **Avoid Moisture:** Diatomaceous earth loses its
effectiveness when it gets wet, so it's best to apply it
in dry conditions.

5. **Limitations:** Diatomaceous earth is primarily effective
against crawling insects and pests. It is less effective against
flying insects and has no residual effect, meaning it needs to
be reapplied after exposure to moisture or when it has been
swept or vacuumed away.

It's important to follow the instructions provided on the
diatomaceous earth product packaging and take necessary
precautions when using it. While DE is considered relatively
safe for humans and pets, it's always a good idea to consult
the specific product label or seek professional advice if you
have concerns or specific questions about its use.

Dust Baths:
     Chickens naturally take dust baths to keep
their feathers clean and free of parasites. Providing a
designated area with loose soil, sand, and wood ash allows

chickens to dust themselves, which helps control external parasites.

A dust bath is a natural behavior exhibited by chickens to maintain their feather and skin health. It involves chickens rolling and fluffing their feathers in loose, dry material to create a dust cloud that they then vigorously shake and bathe in. Dust baths serve several important purposes for chickens:

1. **Cleaning Feathers:** Chickens use dust baths to remove dirt, dust, oils, and parasites from their feathers. The fine particles in the dust effectively absorb excess oils and help break up any debris that may be stuck to the feathers.

2. **Controlling External Parasites:** Dust baths help control external parasites such as mites, lice, and fleas. The dust particles can suffocate and smother these pests, disrupting their life cycle and reducing their numbers on the chicken's body.

3. **Skin Health:** Dust baths also contribute to the overall skin health of chickens. As they bathe in the dust, it reaches the skin, helping to remove dead skin cells, relieve itching, and provide relief from irritation caused by parasites.

To provide a dust bath for your chickens, follow these steps:

1. **Choose a Suitable Area:** Select a designated area in your chicken run or coop where you can create a dust bath.

Ideally, it should be a dry, well-drained spot that won't turn into mud when wet.

2. **Prepare the Dust Bath Material:** The dust bath material should consist of dry, loose, and fine-textured substances. Common options include sand, fine dirt, wood ash, or a mixture of sand and diatomaceous earth. You can also add some dry herbs like mint, lavender, or thyme, as they can provide additional benefits.

3. **Create the Dust Bath Pit:** Dig a shallow pit or use a container large enough for a chicken to comfortably fit in. The pit should be wide and deep enough for chickens to fluff and roll in without making a mess outside the designated area.

4. **Fill the Pit:** Fill the pit or container with the chosen dust bath material. Ensure it's deep enough for chickens to immerse themselves fully.

5. **Encourage and Maintain the Dust Bath:** Introduce your chickens to the dust bath area by gently guiding them or placing them near it. Chickens will instinctively begin to scratch, fluff their feathers, and bathe in the dust. Allow them free access to the dust bath area at all times, ensuring it remains dry and replenishing the material as needed. Providing a dust bath for your chickens allows them to engage in natural behaviors while promoting their health and well-being. It's a simple and enjoyable addition to their

environment

Dosage

The dosage or amount of natural remedies to use for chickens can vary depending on the specific remedy, the size and age of the chickens, and the purpose for which it is being used. It's important to follow the instructions and guidelines provided by reputable sources, such as poultry health experts, experienced chicken keepers, or veterinary professionals. Here are some general considerations:

1. **Recommended Dosage:** Natural remedies often come with recommended dosage guidelines specific to the remedy and its intended use. These guidelines may include measurements such as teaspoons, tablespoons, or milliliters per gallon of water or per specific amount of feed. Always follow the recommended dosage instructions provided by the product manufacturer or reliable sources.

2. **Adjust for Chicken Size and Age:** Consider the size and

age of your chickens when determining the dosage. Young chicks may require lower dosages compared to adult chickens. Adjust the dosage accordingly to ensure it is appropriate for the age and size of your flock.

3. **Start with Small Amounts:** When using natural remedies for the first time, it's generally advisable to start with small amounts and gradually increase if needed. This allows you to observe the chickens' response and assess any potential adverse effects. It's always better to start with a lower dosage and monitor the chickens' well-being before increasing the dosage, if necessary.

4. **Consult Reputable Sources:** Consult reliable sources for dosage guidelines specific to the natural remedy you are using. Reputable poultry health books, poultry websites, experienced chicken keepers or poultry veterinarians can provide valuable guidance on dosage recommendations for specific natural remedies.

5. **Seek Professional Advice:** If you are unsure about the appropriate dosage or if you are dealing with a specific health issue, it's best to consult with a poultry veterinarian or knowledgeable poultry expert. They can provide accurate advice and dosage recommendations based on the specific circumstances of your flock.

Remember, natural remedies should be used judiciously and in conjunction with good husbandry practices. If you have concerns or questions about dosage or the appropriate use of natural remedies, it's always best to seek professional guidance.

It's important to note that while natural remedies can be beneficial in certain situations, they may not be a substitute for proper veterinary care or addressing serious health issues. It's always advisable to consult with a poultry veterinarian or experienced poultry expert for accurate diagnosis and appropriate treatment options

ECHINACEA

E chinacea, also known as purple coneflower, is a popular herb widely recognized for its potential immune-boosting properties.

Here's some information about Echinacea:

1. **Varieties:** There are several species of Echinacea, but the most commonly used ones are Echinacea purpurea, Echinacea angustifolia, and Echinacea pallida.

2. **Medicinal Uses:** Echinacea is primarily known for its potential immune-stimulating effects. It is believed to enhance the activity of the immune system, helping the body fight off infections and shorten the duration of illnesses like the common cold and respiratory infections. Some people also use Echinacea to relieve symptoms of seasonal allergies.

3. **Preparation and Consumption:** Echinacea is available in various forms, including dried herb, liquid extracts, capsules, and teas. It can be taken orally as a supplement or brewed as a tea. Follow the instructions on the product label or consult a healthcare professional for appropriate dosages.

Ectoparasites

E ctoparasites are external parasites that can cause discomfort, irritation, and health issues in chickens. Recognizing the causes and implementing natural remedies is crucial in managing these pests and ensuring the well-being of your flock. In this chapter, we'll delve into the intricacies of ectoparasites, from their origins to effective natural treatment options.

Understanding Ectoparasites:

Ectoparasites are organisms that live on the exterior of their host, feeding on blood, skin, or feathers. Common ectoparasites in chickens include mites, lice, ticks, and fleas. These pests can lead to a range of clinical signs, including feather loss, skin irritation, anemia, and decreased egg production.

Common Ectoparasites in Chickens:

1. Mites:

- **Types:** Red mites, northern fowl mites, scaly leg mites.

- **Effects:** Mites feed on blood and can cause anemia, irritation, and stress in chickens.

2. **Lice:**

- ○ **Types:** Shaft lice, body lice, head lice.

- ○ **Effects:** Lice feed on skin debris and feathers, leading to feather loss, skin irritation, and anemia.

3. **Ticks:**

- ○ **Types:** Soft ticks, hard ticks.

- ○ **Effects:** Ticks feed on blood and can transmit diseases, leading to anemia and potential health issues.

4. **Fleas:**

- ○ **Types:** Sticktight fleas, bird fleas.

- ○ **Effects:** Fleas can cause skin irritation, feather loss, and stress in chickens.

Causes of Ectoparasites:

1. **Poor Sanitation:**

- ○ **Explanation:** Dirty coops and nesting areas create an ideal environment for ectoparasites to thrive.

2. **Infested Environment:**

- ○ **Explanation:** Exposure to contaminated areas or introduction of infested birds can introduce ectoparasites to the flock.

3. **Stress and Weak Immunity:**

- o **Explanation:** Stressed or immunocompromised chickens are more susceptible to ectoparasite infestations.

Natural Remedies for Ectoparasites:
1. **Diatomaceous Earth:**

- o **Benefits:** Diatomaceous earth is a natural desiccant that can be used to kill mites, lice, and other ectoparasites.

- o **Application:** Dust the coop, nesting boxes, and chickens with food-grade diatomaceous earth.

2. **Neem Oil:**

- o **Benefits:** Neem oil has natural insecticidal properties and can help repel and kill ectoparasites.

- o **Application:** Dilute neem oil with water and spray it on the coop and birds.

3. **Herbs and Plants:**

- o **Benefits:** Plants like mint, lavender, and marigold have natural insect-repelling properties.

- o **Application:** Plant these herbs around the coop or use them in nesting material.

4. **Essential Oils:**

- o **Benefits:** Certain essential oils like lavender, tea tree, and eucalyptus have natural insecticidal properties.

- **Application:** Mix a few drops of essential oil with a carrier oil and apply it to affected areas.

Ectoparasites can pose a significant threat to poultry health, but with vigilance and natural remedies, their impact can be minimized. Regular monitoring, strict adherence to biosecurity protocols, and prompt treatment are crucial in safeguarding your flock against ectoparasites. By implementing these natural remedies and good husbandry practices, you can promote the well-being and longevity of your chickens.

EGG PRODUCTION

F or poultry keepers, a sudden halt in egg production can be a perplexing and concerning situation. A well-functioning flock typically provides a steady supply of eggs, so when production suddenly stops, it's natural to wonder what might be causing the interruption. In this blog post, we'll explore the common reasons behind a sudden drop in egg production and offer insights on how to address and prevent this issue.

1. **Molting Season:**

   - **Explanation:** Molting is a natural process in which chickens shed and replace their old feathers. During this period, which can last several weeks, hens redirect their energy towards feather growth rather than egg production.

   - **Solution:** Be patient. Once molting is complete, egg production will gradually resume.

2. Stress and Disturbances:

- ○ **Explanation:** Chickens are sensitive creatures, and any significant stressors, such as moving to a new location, introduction of new flock members, or predator encounters, can temporarily disrupt egg-laying.

- ○ **Solution:** Minimize stressors and provide a calm, consistent environment for your chickens. Allow them time to acclimate to changes.

3. Lighting and Seasonal Changes:

- ○ **Explanation:** Chickens' egg-laying cycles are influenced by daylight hours. Shorter days, which occur in the winter, can trigger a natural reduction in egg production.

- ○ **Solution:** Consider providing artificial lighting in the coop to simulate longer days and encourage consistent egg-laying.

4. Age of the Flock:

- ○ **Explanation:** As chickens age, their egg-laying abilities naturally decline. After a few years, hens may lay fewer eggs or stop altogether.

- ○ **Solution:** If your flock is aging, consider adding younger hens to maintain egg production.

5. Broodiness:

- ○ **Explanation:** A broody hen is one that is determined to sit on a clutch of eggs and hatch them. During this period, broody hens will stop laying eggs.

- ○ **Solution:** If you don't intend to hatch eggs, gently break the broody behavior by providing a separate space and discouraging nest sitting.

6. **Health Issues:**

- ○ **Explanation:** Illness or nutritional deficiencies can impact egg production. Conditions like infectious diseases, parasites, or inadequate diet can lead to a sudden drop in egg-laying.

- ○ **Solution:** Regularly monitor the health of your flock and consult a veterinarian if you suspect any health issues.

7. **Overcrowding:**

- ○ **Explanation:** Overcrowded living conditions can lead to stress, which in turn affects egg production. Chickens need adequate space to move around comfortably.

- ○ **Solution:** Ensure your coop provides ample space for each bird and consider expanding if necessary.

A sudden halt in egg production can be concerning, but it's important to remember that there are various natural factors that can cause this phenomenon. By understanding these potential causes and implementing appropriate solutions, you can help ensure a healthy and productive flock. Regular monitoring, attentive care, and a well-maintained coop are key to resolving and preventing disruptions in egg production.

EGG-RELATED ISSUES

C hickens may experience problems
with egg-laying, such as soft-shelled eggs, shell-less eggs,
egg binding (unable to lay eggs), or prolapse (when the
oviduct protrudes from the vent). Egg binding, a condition
where a hen is unable to pass an egg, is a serious and
potentially life-threatening condition in chickens. It requires
immediate attention and veterinary care.
While natural remedies can sometimes be helpful in mild
cases, it is crucial to seek professional assistance.

However, here are some natural remedies that can be used
in conjunction with veterinary care:

1. **Warm Bath:** Gently placing the affected hen in a warm
bath can help relax the muscles and potentially facilitate the
passage of the egg. Ensure the water temperature is around

105°F (40°C), and keep the hen in the bath for 10-15 minutes.

2. **Lubrication:** Applying a water-based lubricant or petroleum jelly around the vent area may help ease the passage of the egg. Be cautious not to push on the egg or apply excessive force, as it can cause harm.

3.**Calcium and Vitamin D3:** Adequate calcium levels are essential for proper eggshell formation and muscle function. Provide a calcium supplement, such as crushed eggshells or oyster shell, along with a source of Vitamin D3 to aid in calcium absorption. Consult a veterinarian for appropriate dosage instructions.

4. **Gentle Massage:** Lightly massaging the hen's abdomen in a circular motion can help stimulate contractions and potentially assist with egg passage. Be gentle and cautious to avoid causing additional stress or injury.

5. **Moist Heat:** Applying a warm, moist compress to the vent area may help relax the muscles and provide some relief. Use a clean cloth soaked in warm water, ensuring it's not too hot, and gently hold it against the vent for a few minutes. Remember, these natural remedies should not replace professional veterinary care. Egg binding can be a severe condition requiring medical intervention, including manual egg removal, fluids, and potentially hormone injections. If you suspect a hen is egg bound, it is crucial to seek immediate veterinary assistance for proper diagnosis and

treatment

EPSOM SaLT

E psom salt, also known as magnesium sulfate, is a naturally occurring compound that has various uses and potential benefits. Here are some common uses and benefits of Epsom salt:

1. **Bathing and Relaxation:** Epsom salt is often used in baths to promote relaxation and relieve muscle tension. Dissolving Epsom salt in warm bathwater allows the magnesium and sulfate ions to be absorbed through the skin, which may help soothe muscles, reduce stress, and promote a sense of relaxation.

2. **Foot Soaks:** Similar to bath soaks, Epsom salt foot soaks can help relieve tired and achy feet. Soaking your feet in warm water with Epsom salt may provide temporary relief from foot pain, swelling, and foot odor.

3. **Body Scrubs and Exfoliation:** Epsom salt can be combined with oils or other ingredients to create homemade body scrubs. The coarse texture of Epsom salt helps exfoliate the skin, removing dead cells and leaving it feeling smooth and refreshed.

4. **Splinter Removal:** Soaking a splinter in warm water with Epsom salt may help draw it out and ease the removal process. The warm water and Epsom salt can help reduce inflammation and swelling around the affected area

EPSOM SaLT BaTH

An Epsom salt bath can be beneficial for chickens in certain situations, such as providing relief from external parasites, soothing skin irritations, or helping with certain health conditions.

Here's a step-by-step guide on how to give a chicken an Epsom salt bath:

1. **Prepare the bath area:** Find a suitable container or basin that is large enough to comfortably accommodate the chicken. It should be shallow enough that the chicken can stand in it without being submerged too deeply. Ensure the bath area is in a quiet and calm environment.

2. **Fill the container with warm water:** Fill the container with warm water, ensuring it is not too hot or cold. The water

should be comfortably warm to the touch, similar to the temperature of a warm bath.

3. **Dissolve Epsom salt in the water:** Add Epsom salt to the water and stir gently until it is completely dissolved. The recommended amount is approximately 1/2 to 1 cup of Epsom salt per gallon of water, but you can adjust the quantity depending on the size of the container and the specific needs of the chicken.

4. **Introduce the chicken to the bath:** Gently place the chicken into the water, making sure it is standing comfortably and not struggling. Hold the chicken securely but avoid applying excessive pressure.

5. **Allow the chicken to soak:** Allow the chicken to stand in the Epsom salt bath for about 10-15 minutes. This gives the Epsom salt time to work and allows the chicken to relax.

6. **Monitor the chicken:** While the chicken is in the bath, keep a close eye on its behavior and overall comfort. If the chicken becomes excessively stressed or shows signs of distress, such as panting or struggling, remove it from the bath immediately.

7. Rinse the chicken (optional): After the soaking period, you can rinse the chicken with clean, lukewarm water to remove any residual Epsom salt. This step is optional and may not be necessary depending on the situation and the specific instructions provided by a veterinarian.

8. Dry the chicken: Gently lift the chicken out of the bath and place it on a clean, dry towel or in a warm, draft-free area. Pat the chicken's feathers dry using the towel, ensuring it is kept warm to prevent chilling.

It's important to note that while Epsom salt baths can provide certain benefits, they should be used judiciously and only when necessary. It's advisable to consult with a veterinarian for guidance on the specific use of Epsom salt baths for your chicken's condition or situation, as they can provide tailored advice based on the chicken's health and needs

Essential Oils

U nderstanding Essential Oils:

Essential oils are concentrated extracts derived from plants through processes like steam distillation or cold pressing. They are packed with the natural compounds and aromatic properties of their source plants, making them highly potent and effective.

Benefits of Essential Oils for Chickens:

1. **Antimicrobial Properties:**

Essential oils such as tea tree, oregano, and thyme possess powerful antimicrobial properties. They can help combat common pathogens and keep your flock healthy.

2. **Stress Reduction:**

Lavender, chamomile, and clary sage essential oils have calming effects. These can be especially useful during times of stress, such as introducing new birds to the flock or dealing with environmental changes.

3. **Respiratory Support:**

Eucalyptus and peppermint essential oils can assist in maintaining clear airways and supporting respiratory health, especially in colder months.

4. Insect Repellent:

Oils like citronella, lemongrass, and cedarwood are natural insect repellents. They can help protect your chickens from pests like mites and fleas.

Safe Usage Guidelines:

Before incorporating essential oils into your poultry care routine, it's crucial to follow these guidelines:

1. Dilution:

Essential oils are highly concentrated and should always be diluted before use. A general rule of thumb is to mix 1-2 drops of essential oil with a carrier oil like coconut or olive oil.

2. Avoid Eye Contact:

Be cautious when applying oils near the eyes or sensitive areas of your chickens.

3. Test for Sensitivity:

Before applying a new oil, perform a patch test on a small area of your chicken's skin to ensure there are no adverse reactions.

Applications for Chickens:

1. Aromatherapy:

Diffusing essential oils in the coop can create a calming atmosphere. Lavender and chamomile are excellent choices for relaxation.

2. **Topical Applications:**

Create a diluted oil blend to rub on your chicken's feet, legs, or chest. This can be helpful for promoting respiratory health or soothing sore muscles.

3. **Cleaning Solutions:**

Make a natural coop cleaner by mixing water, vinegar, and a few drops of citrus or tea tree oil. This will help keep the environment sanitary and pest-free.

4. **Misting:**

Blend essential oils with water and use a spray bottle to mist the coop or nesting area. This can help deter insects and maintain a clean, pleasant environment.

By incorporating essential oils into your chicken care routine, you can enhance the well-being and overall health of your flock. Remember to approach their usage with care and always prioritize safety. With the right knowledge and application, essential oils can be a valuable asset in your quest for happy, thriving chickens.

Eye Infections

Identifying Eye Irritations and Infections

Vigilance is key when it comes to your chickens' ocular health. Keep an eye out for signs such as redness, swelling, excessive blinking, discharge, or cloudiness in their eyes. These could be indicators of irritations or infections caused by foreign particles, dust, bacteria, viruses, or even injury.

Gentle Cleaning and First Aid

If you notice any of the above symptoms, it's time to step in with gentle cleaning and first aid. Prepare a saline solution by mixing a teaspoon of salt in a cup of warm water. Using a clean cloth or cotton ball, carefully wipe away any debris or discharge from the affected eye. Be patient and avoid causing further stress to your chicken.

Herbal Solutions for Relief

Nature often provides effective remedies for common ailments, and chicken eye irritations are no exception. Herbal treatments like chamomile tea, calendula oil, or aloe vera gel can provide relief and promote healing. These natural options can be used to gently cleanse the eye and soothe any discomfort.

Veterinary Consultation

For persistent or severe eye issues, consulting a poultry veterinarian is crucial. They can accurately diagnose the problem and prescribe appropriate medications if necessary. Timely intervention can prevent further complications and ensure your chickens receive the care they need.

Preventing Eye Irritations and Infections

Prevention is always preferable to treatment. To minimize the risk of eye issues in your flock, consider these preventive measures:

Clean and Dry Coop: Maintain a clean and dry coop environment to reduce the chances of dust and particles causing irritations.

Dust Bath: Provide your chickens with a designated dust-bathing area to help them naturally clean their feathers and eyes.

Good Ventilation: Ensure proper ventilation in the coop to minimize moisture and prevent the buildup of ammonia, which can irritate eyes.

Routine Health Checks: Regularly inspect your chickens' eyes as part of routine health checks, and address any issues promptly.

Caring for Healthy Eyes and Happy Chickens

Treating and preventing eye irritations and infections in chickens requires a delicate balance of observation, proactive measures, and appropriate interventions. By staying attuned to your chickens' well-being, providing gentle care, and seeking professional guidance when needed, you're not just safeguarding their ocular health – you're nurturing a happy and thriving flock that can continue to grace your backyard with their vibrant presence. Remember, healthy eyes lead to happy clucks!

FLIES

For chicken owners, a clean and healthy coop is essential for the well-being of your feathered friends. One of the most common challenges in maintaining a coop's hygiene is managing flies. These pests not only irritate your chickens but can also spread disease. In this post, we'll explore effective strategies to help chicken owners keep their coops free from bothersome flies.

Maintain a Clean Environment:

Regularly clean the coop to remove droppings, spoiled feed, and any damp bedding. Flies are attracted to decaying organic matter, so keeping the area clean is the first line of defense.

Proper Waste Management:

Use a deep litter method with materials like straw, wood shavings, or hay. This helps absorb moisture and control odors, reducing the attraction for flies.

Implement Good Ventilation:

Adequate airflow helps keep the coop dry and discourages fly breeding. Ensure windows, vents, and openings are properly screened to prevent unwanted pests from entering.

Install Fly Screens or Nets:

Cover coop windows and vents with fine-mesh screens or nets to create a barrier against flies while still allowing for ventilation.

Utilize Natural Predators:

Introduce natural predators like chickens, ducks, or even certain types of predatory insects (like ladybugs) that feed on fly larvae and eggs.

Apply Diatomaceous Earth (DE):

DE is a natural powder that can be sprinkled around the coop. It's harmless to chickens but lethal to insects due to its abrasive texture.

Utilize Herbs and Plants:

Planting herbs like basil, mint, or lavender around the coop can act as natural repellents for flies.

Limit Standing Water:

Ensure there are no stagnant water sources near the coop, as they can serve as breeding grounds for flies.

Use Fly Traps or Sticky Tape:

Hanging fly traps or strips of sticky tape can help capture adult flies, reducing their population.

Regularly Rotate Compost Piles:

If you have a compost pile near the coop, turn it regularly to prevent fly breeding in the decomposing material.

Consider Biological Controls:

Beneficial nematodes or parasitic wasps can be introduced to control fly larvae in the soil.

By implementing these strategies, chicken owners can effectively manage flies in their coops, creating a healthier and more comfortable environment for their feathered companions. Remember, a proactive approach to coop maintenance and pest control will not only benefit your chickens but also contribute to a more enjoyable and sustainable backyard poultry experience. Here's to fly-free coops and happy, healthy hens!

FLOCK SIZE

The number of chickens you should have depends on several factors, including your specific goals, available space, local regulations, and your capacity to care for them properly.

Here are some considerations to help you determine the appropriate number of chickens for your situation:

1. **Purpose:** Consider your purpose for keeping chickens. Are you primarily interested in eggs, meat, pest control, or simply as pets? Different purposes may require different numbers of chickens. For example, if you want a steady supply of eggs for personal consumption, a smaller flock of 3-5 chickens may be sufficient. If you're raising chickens for meat, you might consider a larger flock.

2. **Space:** Evaluate the available space you have for your chickens. Chickens need adequate space to roam, exercise,

and engage in natural behaviors. Ideally, they should have access to a secure coop and a run or free-range area. The recommended space per chicken varies, but a general guideline is at least 4 square feet per bird in the coop and 10 square feet per bird in the run or free-range area.

3. **Local regulations:** Check your local regulations or zoning laws to determine if there are any restrictions on the number of chickens allowed in your area. Some municipalities have specific guidelines regarding flock size, noise regulations, and proximity to neighboring properties.

4. **Time and Effort:** Consider the time and effort you can dedicate to caring for your chickens. Raising chickens requires daily care, including feeding, watering, cleaning the coop, and monitoring their health. A larger flock may require more time and effort to manage effectively.

5. **Sustainability:** Ensure that you can sustainably provide for the needs of your flock. This includes supplying appropriate feed, clean water, and proper healthcare. Overcrowding can lead to stress, health issues, and reduced productivity.

6. **Future Expansion:** Consider your future plans. If you anticipate expanding your flock in the future, it may be prudent to start with a smaller number of chickens and gradually increase as you gain experience and confidence. It's always a good idea to start small and gradually increase

your flock size as you become more comfortable and knowledgeable about chicken care.

Remember to provide a
suitable environment, proper nutrition, and routine veterinary care to ensure the health and well-being of your chickens

FLOOrING FOr COOP

Selecting the ideal flooring for your chicken coop is a crucial decision that can significantly impact the health, cleanliness, and overall well-being of your flock. In this comprehensive guide, we'll explore the best types of flooring options for chicken coops, weighing the pros and cons of each to help you make an informed choice.

1. **Dirt or Soil Flooring:**

   ○ **Pros:**

     - Natural and cost-effective option.

     - Allows for natural dust bathing behavior.

     - Provides a comfortable surface for chickens to scratch and forage.

   ○ **Cons:**

     - Requires regular maintenance and replenishing to prevent holes and uneven surfaces.

- Susceptible to erosion and muddy conditions in wet weather.

2. Concrete Flooring:

- Pros:

  - Durable and long-lasting, providing a solid surface that's easy to clean.

  - Helps deter pests and predators from burrowing into the coop.

  - Reduces the risk of bacterial growth and disease transmission.

- Cons:

  - May be uncomfortable for chickens to walk on for extended periods, potentially leading to foot pad issues.

  - Requires proper drainage to prevent pooling of water and subsequent dampness.

3. Sand Flooring:

- Pros:

  - Excellent drainage properties, preventing puddles and promoting dry conditions.

  - Facilitates natural dust bathing behavior.

  - Easy to clean and sift for waste removal.

○ **Cons:**

- Initial setup may require a significant amount of sand.

- Needs regular replenishing to maintain an even surface.

4. **Gravel Flooring:**

○ **Pros:**

- Provides excellent drainage and prevents water pooling.

- Deters pests and predators from digging into the coop.

- Promotes natural foraging behavior.

○ **Cons:**

- Requires a layer of sand or topsoil on top for added comfort.

- Gravel can become compacted and uncomfortable for chickens over time.

5. **Hardware Cloth or Wire Mesh Flooring:**

○ **Pros:**

- Highly effective in deterring predators, including burrowing ones.

- Allows droppings to fall through, keeping the coop cleaner.

  ○ **Cons:**

- Uncomfortable for chickens to walk on for extended periods, potentially leading to foot pad issues.

- Requires additional flooring material on top for comfort.

Choosing the right flooring for your chicken coop is a crucial step in creating a comfortable and healthy environment for your flock. Each type of flooring comes with its own set of advantages and considerations, so it's important to weigh your options based on your specific needs and preferences. Remember, regular maintenance and cleanliness are key to ensuring a happy and thriving flock. With the right flooring in place, your chickens will have a cozy and secure coop to call home.

FUNGUS ON THE COMB

C auses of Fungus on the Comb:

1. **Humid Environments:**
   High humidity levels provide an ideal breeding ground for fungi. Coops with poor ventilation or damp bedding can contribute to fungal growth.

2. **Poor Sanitation Practices:**
   Inadequate cleaning and disinfection of the coop and nesting areas can lead to the proliferation of fungal spores.

3. **Close Quarters and Overcrowding:**
   Overcrowded coops can increase stress levels among chickens, weakening their immune systems and making them more susceptible to fungal infections.

4. **Injury or Irritation:**
   Any form of injury or irritation on the comb can create an entry point for fungi. These infections can also occur sec-

ondary to other conditions like pecking or frostbite.

5. **Contaminated Feeding and Water Sources:**
   Moldy or contaminated feed and water can introduce fungal spores into the digestive system, leading to systemic fungal infections.

Treatment Options for Fungus on the Comb:

1. **Isolation and Quarantine:**
   Immediately separate the affected chicken from the rest of the flock to prevent the spread of the fungus.

2. **Topical Antifungal Treatments:**
   Apply a veterinary-approved antifungal ointment or cream directly to the affected area on the comb. Follow the recommended dosage and application instructions.

3. **Hygiene and Sanitation:**
   Thoroughly clean and disinfect the coop, nesting areas, and feeders to eliminate any fungal spores. Replace bedding material with clean, dry material.

4. **Improve Ventilation:**
   Ensure proper airflow and ventilation within the coop to reduce humidity levels and discourage fungal growth.

5. **Monitor for Signs of Improvement:**
   Keep a close eye on the affected chicken's comb for signs of improvement. If the condition worsens or does not improve within a reasonable timeframe, consult a veterinarian for further guidance.

6. **Provide a Balanced Diet:**

Offer a nutritionally balanced diet to support the chicken's immune system and overall health, aiding in the recovery process.

7. **Preventative Measures:**

Implement preventative measures such as regular cleaning, proper coop ventilation, and maintaining optimal flock size to reduce the risk of future fungal infections.

Fungal infections on a chicken's comb can be successfully managed with prompt identification and appropriate treatment. By understanding the causes and implementing effective remedies, you can help your chicken recover and prevent future occurrences. Remember, consulting a veterinarian for professional advice is always recommended in severe or persistent cases. With proper care and attention, your flock will thrive in a healthy and fungus-free environment.

Garlic

Here are some natural uses for garlic:

1. **Immune Support:** Garlic is believed to have immune-boosting properties. It contains compounds, such as allicin, which may help stimulate the immune system and enhance its ability to fight off infections and diseases.

2. **Cardiovascular Health:** Garlic has been associated with potential cardiovascular benefits. It may help lower blood pressure, reduce cholesterol levels, and improve overall heart health. Regular consumption of garlic, as part of a balanced diet, may support cardiovascular well-being.

3. **Anti-Inflammatory Effects:** Garlic contains anti-inflammatory compounds that may help reduce inflammation in the body. This can be beneficial for

conditions such as arthritis and other inflammatory disorders.

4. **Antimicrobial Properties:** Garlic has antimicrobial properties, thanks to its active compounds like allicin. It may have potential antibacterial, antiviral, and antifungal effects. Some people use garlic topically to help with minor skin infections or fungal conditions like athlete's foot.

5. **Natural Insect Repellent:** Garlic has a strong odor that repels some insects. You can create a natural insect repellent spray by blending garlic with water and applying it to plants or around the desired area to deter pests.

6. **Garden Pest Control:** Garlic is believed to have properties that can help repel certain garden pests like aphids, snails, and slugs. Planting garlic among susceptible plants or using garlic-based sprays may help protect your garden.

Garlic is known for its natural antibacterial and antiparasitic properties. Adding crushed or powdered garlic to their feed or mixing it with water can help deter parasites and support immune function.

Heat Exhaustion

Recognizing Signs of Heat Exhaustion:

1. **Lethargy and Weakness:**

   Chickens experiencing heat exhaustion will often appear sluggish and weak. They may be reluctant to move and may even have difficulty standing.

2. **Heavy Panting and Rapid Breathing:**

   Excessive panting is a clear indication that a chicken is struggling to regulate its body temperature. This can be accompanied by rapid, shallow breathing.

3. **Pale Comb and Wattles:**

   The comb and wattles of a heat-stressed chicken may become pale or even bluish in color due to reduced blood flow and circulation.

4. **Drooping Wings and Tail Feathers:**

   Chickens suffering from heat exhaustion may extend their

wings and tail feathers in an attempt to dissipate heat.

5. **Loss of Appetite and Reduced Water Consumption:**
   Heat-stressed chickens may lose interest in food and water, leading to dehydration.

6. **Laying Abnormalities:**
   High temperatures can disrupt egg production, leading to soft-shelled or irregularly laid eggs.

Remedies for Heat Exhaustion:

1. **Provide Immediate Shade and Ventilation:**
   Move affected chickens to a shaded area with good airflow. Ensure there are no obstructions preventing air circulation.

2. **Offer Fresh, Cool Water:**
   Provide chickens with access to fresh, cool water. Adding electrolytes to the water can help replenish essential minerals lost through heat stress.

3. **Cooling Soaks or Misting:**
   Gently misting or offering a shallow container of cool water for chickens to wade in can help lower their body temperature.

4. **Frozen Treats and Watermelon:**
   Treats like frozen fruits or watermelon chunks provide both hydration and a refreshing source of nutrients.

5. **Avoid Handling:**
   Minimize handling of heat-exhausted chickens, as this can cause additional stress.

6. **Limit Activity:**

Encourage affected chickens to rest and minimize any unnecessary movement.

7. **Monitor Progress:**

Keep a close eye on the chickens' behavior and vital signs. If their condition does not improve, seek professional veterinary advice immediately.

Prevention is Key:

To prevent heat exhaustion in the first place, consider the following proactive measures:

- Ensure access to shaded areas and proper ventilation in the coop.

- Provide multiple water sources and consider using automatic watering systems.

- Avoid handling chickens during the hottest parts of the day.

- Install fans or misting systems in the coop for added cooling.

Recognizing the signs of heat exhaustion and acting promptly with effective remedies is crucial in ensuring the well-being of your chickens during hot weather. By implementing proactive measures and staying vigilant, you can help your flock stay cool, comfortable, and healthy even in the midst of a heatwave.

Herbal Coop Bedding

The Benefits of Herbal Coop Bedding:

1. **Natural Pest Deterrent:**

   Certain herbs like mint, lavender, and rosemary possess natural insect-repelling properties. Placing them in the coop bedding can help deter pests and protect your chickens from potential infestations.

2. **Antibacterial and Antifungal Properties:**

   Herbs like oregano and thyme contain compounds that have antibacterial and antifungal properties. Using these herbs in the bedding can help maintain a cleaner and healthier coop environment.

3. **Aromatherapy for Stress Reduction:**

   Lavender, chamomile, and lemon balm are known for their calming and stress-reducing properties. These herbs can create a soothing atmosphere for your chickens, promoting a sense of calm and well-being.

4. **Improved Respiratory Health:**

Herbs such as eucalyptus and peppermint release aromatic compounds that can support respiratory health. This is particularly beneficial in preventing respiratory issues in your flock.

Selecting Herbs for Coop Bedding:

1. **Lavender (Lavandula spp.):**

Known for its calming properties, lavender is a popular choice for coop bedding. Its pleasant scent can help create a tranquil environment for your chickens.

2. **Mint (Mentha spp.):**

Mint varieties like peppermint and spearmint have potent insect-repelling qualities. They can also add a refreshing scent to the coop.

3. **Oregano (Origanum vulgare):**

Oregano contains natural compounds with antibacterial and antifungal properties. Including it in the bedding can contribute to a cleaner and healthier coop.

4. **Thyme (Thymus vulgaris):**

Thyme is another herb with strong antibacterial properties. It can help create an environment that supports optimal health for your chickens.

Application of Herbal Coop Bedding:

1. **Drying and Preparation:**

Harvest fresh herbs and allow them to air dry thoroughly. Once dried, crush or chop them to release their aromatic compounds.

2. **Mixing with Bedding Material:**

Combine the dried herbs with your preferred bedding material, such as straw or wood shavings. Ensure an even distribution for maximum effectiveness.

3. **Regular Refreshing:**

Over time, the aromatic properties of the herbs may diminish. It's advisable to refresh the coop bedding with a new batch of dried herbs periodically.

Conclusion:

Herbal coop bedding offers a natural and aromatic way to enhance the comfort and well-being of your chickens. By carefully selecting and incorporating herbs known for their beneficial properties, you can create a coop environment that promotes health, relaxation, and happiness for your feathered friends. Remember, a contented and stress-free flock leads to healthier, happier hens!

Herbal Coop Sprays

C reating a natural coop spray by steeping herbs like lavender, thyme, or rosemary in water and spraying it inside the coop can help repel pests and promote a clean and fresh environment.

How do you make an herbal coop spray?
Making an herbal coop spray is a straightforward process. Here's a simple recipe to create your own herbal coop spray:

Ingredients:
• cups of water
• 2 tablespoons of dried herbs (such as lavender, thyme, rosemary, mint, or a combination)
• Optional: 1-2 tablespoons of apple cider vinegar (for added antimicrobial properties)
Instructions:
1. Boil the water in a pot.
2. Once the water comes to a boil, remove it from the

heat.

3. Add the dried herbs to the hot water.

4. Cover the pot and let the herbs steep in the water for at least 30 minutes or until the water has cooled.

5. Strain the mixture to remove the herbs, using a finemesh strainer or cheesecloth.

6. If desired, add 1-2 tablespoons of apple cider vinegar to the strained liquid and stir well. The vinegar can provide additional antimicrobial properties.

7. Pour the herbal mixture into a clean spray bottle or container.

8. Label the container with the contents and date.

To Use:

1. Shake the spray bottle well before each use.

2. Spray the herbal mixture inside the coop, paying attention to cracks, corners, perches, and nesting boxes.

3. You can also spray the mixture directly on the chickens' feathers, avoiding the head and eyes.

4. Repeat the application as needed, or whenever you notice signs of pests or to freshen the coop.

Note: While herbal coop sprays can help repel pests and create a pleasant environment, they may not eliminate an existing infestation. If you suspect a severe pest problem, it's advisable to consult with a poultry veterinarian or expert for appropriate treatment options.

Additionally, it's important to consider the individual sensitivities of your chickens. Some chickens may be more sensitive to certain herbs or essential oils, so monitor their behavior and well-being after using any

new product. If you observe any adverse reactions,
discontinue use immediately

Herbs

Certain herbs have beneficial properties for chickens. For example:

1. **Oregano:** Oregano has antimicrobial properties and can be added to feed or provided in their coop to support respiratory health and boost immunity.
2. **Thyme:** Thyme is known for its antimicrobial and antiparasitic properties, and it can be used in the coop bedding or added to their diet.
3. **Mint:** Mint can help deter pests and has a calming effect on chickens.
4. **Calendula:** Calendula flowers have antimicrobial properties and can be added to the feed or used in salves for skin irritations.

Marek's Disease

Marek's disease is a viral disease that affects young chickens. It can cause paralysis, weight loss, poor growth, eye irregularities, and tumors in various organs. It is highly contagious and can lead to high mortality rates. Marek's disease is a highly contagious and devastating viral disease that primarily affects chickens. It is caused by the Marek's disease virus (MDV), which belongs to the herpesvirus family. Marek's disease primarily affects young chickens between the ages of 3 and 16 weeks, but it can also affect older birds.

Here are some key characteristics and effects of Marek's disease:

1. **Transmission:** Marek's disease is primarily transmitted through the shedding of virus particles from infected birds. The virus is shed through dander, feather follicles, and

bodily fluids. It can survive in the environment for months, making it highly contagious and easily spread between birds.

2. **Symptoms:** The symptoms of Marek's disease can vary depending on the affected organs and the strain of the virus. Common symptoms include paralysis or weakness in the legs, wings, or neck, weight loss, loss of appetite, eye changes (gray or irregular pupils), labored breathing, and tumor formation in internal organs.

3. **Tumors:** Marek's disease can cause the formation of tumors, primarily in the nerves, skin, internal organs, and sometimes the eyes. These tumors can disrupt the normal functioning of affected organs and systems, leading to various health issues.

4. **Immunosuppression:** Marek's disease can suppress the chicken's immune system, making them more susceptible to secondary infections and reducing their ability to fight off diseases. This immunosuppression can have long-lasting effects on the bird's overall health.

5. **High Mortality:** Marek's disease can cause high mortality rates in affected flocks, especially in unvaccinated birds or those with weakened immune systems. Mortality rates can range from a few birds to significant losses in a flock.

6. **Vaccination:** Vaccination is a crucial preventive measure against Marek's disease. Commercial vaccines are available and are commonly administered to chicks at an early age to provide immunity against the virus. Vaccination helps reduce the severity of the disease, decreases tumor formation, and prevents widespread outbreaks.

It's important to note that Marek's disease is not zoonotic, which means it cannot be transmitted to humans. However, it poses a significant threat to the poultry industry and backyard chicken flocks. If you suspect Marek's disease in your chickens, it's essential to contact a poultry veterinarian for diagnosis, guidance on managing the disease, and prevention strategies for your flock.

There are currently no known natural remedies or treatments for Marek's disease in chickens. Marek's disease is a viral infection caused by the Marek's disease virus (MDV), and it requires a comprehensive approach for prevention and management. The best course of action is to focus on preventative measures and good husbandry practices to minimize the impact of the disease.

Here are some Recommendations:

1. Vaccination: Vaccination is the most effective method for preventing Marek's disease in chickens. Commercial vaccines are available and should be administered to chicks at a young age according to the manufacturer's instructions. Vaccination can significantly reduce the severity of the disease and help protect the flock.

2. Biosecurity: Implement strict biosecurity measures to prevent the introduction and spread of the virus. This includes maintaining a clean and sanitized environment, limiting visitors, quarantining new birds, and preventing contact with wild birds or other poultry flocks.

3. Genetic Selection: Some chicken breeds and genetic lines may be more resistant to Marek's disease than others.

Consider selecting chicken breeds or lines that have been bred for increased resistance to the disease.

4. Sanitation and Hygiene: Practice good coop hygiene by regularly cleaning and disinfecting the living areas, equipment, and water sources. This helps reduce the potential for virus transmission and minimizes the risk of infection.

5. Stress Reduction: High stress levels can weaken the immune system and make chickens more susceptible to infections. Provide a low-stress environment for your chickens with proper housing, adequate space, balanced nutrition, access to clean water, and minimal disruptions.

6. Quarantine and Monitoring: Quarantine new birds before introducing them to the existing flock. Monitor the health of your chickens regularly and be vigilant for any signs or symptoms of Marek's disease. Isolate and seek veterinary assistance for any birds displaying suspicious symptoms.

It's important to note that Marek's disease is a complex and challenging disease to manage. If you suspect Marek's disease or have concerns about the health of your flock, it is recommended to consult with a poultry veterinarian or experienced poultry professional for an accurate diagnosis and appropriate management strategies

MITES

Are common external parasites that can affect chickens. There are different types of mites that can infest chickens, including red mites (Dermanyssus gallinae) and northern fowl mites (Ornithonyssus sylviarum).

Here's some information on mites in chickens:

1. **Symptoms:** Signs of mite infestation in chickens may include feather loss, especially around the vent and under the wings, irritation, restlessness, decreased egg production, pale comb, anemia (pale skin), and visible mites on the bird's skin.

2. **Life Cycle and Habits:** Mites are nocturnal pests that hide during the day and feed on chickens at night. They can live in cracks, crevices, and bedding material in the coop. Mites can survive for several months without feeding, making them difficult to eradicate.

3. **Prevention:** Regular coop maintenance and cleanliness
are essential for preventing mite infestations. Clean and
disinfect the coop regularly, remove any potential hiding
spots for mites, and practice good biosecurity measures.
Quarantine new birds before introducing them to the existing
flock to prevent mite transmission.

4. **Treatment:** If mite infestation is suspected, there are
several treatment options available:

• **Topical Treatments:** Dusting or spraying the
birds and their environment with poultry-friendly
insecticides or natural alternatives can help
control mites
  Permethrin-based products: Some
commercially available products contain
permethrin, which can be applied directly to the
birds or used to treat the coop.
• **Natural Remedies:** Some natural remedies, such
as diatomaceous earth, neem oil, or essential oils,
may be used as part of an integrated pest
management approach. However, it's important
to research and use them properly, as they may
not be as effective as chemical treatments alone.
• **Consult a veterinarian:** If the infestation is
severe or doesn't improve with basic treatments,
it's advisable to consult a veterinarian who can
provide guidance and prescribe appropriate
medications or treatments.

MYCOPLASMA GALLISEPTICUM

M ycoplasma gallisepticum, commonly known as MG, is a bacterial infection that can have significant respiratory effects on chickens. Recognizing the causes and implementing natural remedies is essential in managing this ailment and safeguarding the well-being of your flock. In this chapter, we'll delve into the intricacies of Mycoplasma gallisepticum, from its origins to effective natural treatment options.

Understanding Mycoplasma Gallisepticum:

Mycoplasma gallisepticum is a bacterium that primarily targets the respiratory system of chickens. It can lead to symptoms like coughing, sneezing, nasal discharge, and in severe cases, decreased egg production. MG is highly contagious and can spread rapidly among flocks.

Common Signs of Mycoplasma Gallisepticum:

1. **Respiratory Symptoms:**

   ○ Chickens may exhibit signs such as coughing, sneezing,

and nasal discharge.

2. Swollen Eyes and Sinusitis:

- In severe cases, MG can lead to swollen eyes and sinusitis.

3. Decreased Egg Production:

- Infected hens may experience a sharp decline in egg-laying productivity.

Causes of Mycoplasma Gallisepticum:

1. Close Contact with Infected Birds:

- Chickens can contract MG through direct contact with infected birds or exposure to contaminated environments.

2. Carrier Birds:

- Chickens can carry MG without displaying symptoms, acting as reservoirs and potentially spreading the infection to others.

Natural Remedies for Mycoplasma Gallisepticum:

1. Echinacea:

- **Benefits:** Echinacea is known for its immune-boosting properties. It can help strengthen the immune system, aiding in recovery.

- **Application:** Offer echinacea tincture in their drinking water, following dosage recommendations.

2. **Garlic and Honey:**

- ○ **Benefits:** Garlic has natural antibacterial properties, while honey soothes the throat and supports the immune system.

- ○ **Application:** Crush a clove of garlic and mix it with honey. Administer a small amount as a supplement.

3. **Thyme Infusions:**

- ○ **Benefits:** Thyme has natural antibacterial properties and can help support respiratory health.

- ○ **Application:** Provide thyme-infused water as a drink.

4. **Oregano Oil:**

- ○ **Benefits:** Oregano oil is a powerful natural antibacterial agent.

- ○ **Application:** Dilute oregano oil and add it to their drinking water, following recommended dosage.

5. **Vitamin-Rich Foods:**

- ○ **Benefits:** Provide foods rich in vitamins, especially vitamin C, to support the immune system.

- ○ **Application:** Offer fruits like oranges, berries, and kiwi as treats.

Mycoplasma gallisepticum is a serious bacterial infection that requires prompt attention. While natural remedies can be supportive, it's crucial to consult with a veterinarian for severe cases or if symptoms persist. Combining natural remedies with strict biosecurity measures and a balanced diet will contribute to the overall health and well-being of your flock during this challenging time. With proper care and attention, you can help your chickens recover and prevent future occurrences of Mycoplasma gallisepticum.

Natural Alternatives
TO ANTIBIOTICS

N atural Antibiotics for Chickens:

Raising chickens is a rewarding endeavor, whether for their fresh eggs, companionship, or the simple joy they bring to a backyard. Ensuring the health and well-being of your feathered friends is paramount, and in your quest for their optimal care, you might be interested in exploring natural alternatives to antibiotics. Just as humans have turned to traditional remedies, chickens too can benefit from the power of nature's healing resources. Here's a look at some natural antibiotics that can support your flock's health:

1. **Garlic:** Nature's Immune Booster

Garlic isn't just a culinary delight—it's a powerful immune booster. Adding fresh garlic or garlic powder to your chickens' diet can help strengthen their immune systems and fend off infections. Garlic's natural compounds have been shown to possess antimicrobial and antiviral properties that can be beneficial for your flock.

2. **Apple Cider Vinegar:** The Multi-Purpose Elixir

Apple cider vinegar is renowned for its various health benefits, and chickens are no exception to its positive effects. Adding a small amount of apple cider vinegar to their drinking water can help promote good gut health, aiding in digestion and preventing the growth of harmful bacteria.

3. **Oregano:** The Herbal Defender

Oregano isn't just a flavorful herb for your meals; it's also a natural antibiotic for chickens. Rich in antioxidants and essential oils, oregano has shown antimicrobial properties that can assist in keeping bacterial infections at bay. Adding oregano to their diet or providing them with oregano-infused water can be a proactive measure.

4. **Honey:** A Sweet Solution

Honey has been revered for centuries for its natural healing properties. A small amount of raw, unpasteurized honey can act as a soothing agent for your chickens' throats and help with respiratory issues. Its antibacterial properties make it a valuable addition to their diet.

5. **Probiotics:** Gut Health Guardians

Probiotics are beneficial bacteria that support gut health. Adding probiotics to your chickens' diet can promote a balanced digestive system, enhancing nutrient absorption and boosting their immune systems. You can find poultry-specific probiotics at your local feed store or through online suppliers.

6. **Turmeric:** The Golden Healer

Turmeric's active compound, curcumin, has well-documented anti-inflammatory and antibacterial properties. Adding a sprinkle of turmeric to your chickens' feed can contribute to their overall well-being and help them fight off infections.

7. **Echinacea:** The Herbal Shield

Echinacea is a popular herb known for its immune-boosting qualities. By adding echinacea to their diet, you can provide your chickens with an extra layer of protection against common illnesses.

8. **Neem Oil:** The Natural Repellant

Neem oil isn't just effective against pests; it also possesses antibacterial properties. Incorporating neem oil into your coop maintenance routine can help maintain a clean and hygienic environment for your chickens.

While these natural antibiotics offer valuable support for your chickens' health, it's important to remember that prevention is key. Providing a clean and stress-free living environment, offering a balanced diet, and practicing good biosecurity measures are fundamental to keeping your flock healthy.

As you explore these natural alternatives, consider consulting with a poultry veterinarian or an experienced chicken keeper. Your chickens deserve the best care possible, and incorporating these natural antibiotics can be a step in the right direction, promoting their well-being the natural way.

NESTING BOXES

C leaning nesting boxes is an important task to maintain a clean and hygienic environment for your chickens. Here's a step-by-step guide on how to clean nesting boxes:

1. **Gather the necessary supplies:** Before starting the cleaning process, gather the following supplies:
• Protective gloves
• Face mask (if desired)
• Scraper or spatula
• Broom or brush
• Bucket of warm water
• Mild detergent or poultry-safe disinfectant
• Clean cloth or sponge
• Fresh bedding material (such as straw or wood shavings)

2. **Empty the nesting boxes:** Remove any eggs from the

nesting boxes and place them in a safe location. If any eggs
are cracked or soiled, discard them.

3. **Scrape off debris:** Use a scraper or spatula to remove any
stuck-on debris, dried droppings, or soiled bedding from the
nesting boxes. Be gentle to avoid damaging the nesting
material or the box itself.

4. **Dispose of waste:** Collect the scraped debris and soiled
bedding in a bucket or suitable container for proper disposal.
Consider composting the waste in a designated compost area
if desired.

5. **Brush or sweep the nesting boxes:** Use a broom or brush
to sweep out any remaining dirt or loose particles from the
nesting boxes. Pay attention to corners and crevices where
debris may accumulate.

6. **Prepare a cleaning solution:** Fill a bucket with warm
water and add a mild detergent or poultry-safe disinfectant
according to the manufacturer's instructions. Mix well to
create a cleaning solution

    7. **Clean the nesting boxes:** Dip a clean cloth or sponge into
the cleaning solution and wring out excess moisture.
Use the damp cloth or sponge to wipe down all surfaces of
the nesting boxes, including the floor, sides, and dividers.
Pay extra attention to any areas with visible stains or residue.

8. **Rinse the nesting boxes:** After wiping down the nesting
boxes with the cleaning solution, rinse the surfaces with

clean water to remove any remaining detergent or disinfectant residue.

9. **Allow the nesting boxes to dry:** Leave the nesting boxes open and allow them to air dry completely. Proper ventilation will help expedite the drying process and prevent moisture buildup.

10. **Replace bedding material:** Once the nesting boxes are dry, add a fresh layer of clean bedding material, such as straw or wood shavings, to each nesting box. Ensure the bedding is dry and comfortable for the chickens.

11. **Return eggs to the nesting boxes:** Once the nesting boxes are clean, dry, and filled with fresh bedding, place the clean eggs back into their respective nesting boxes. Regular cleaning of nesting boxes, ideally on a weekly basis, helps maintain a clean and inviting environment for your chickens to lay eggs. It reduces the risk of bacterial contamination and keeps the nesting boxes comfortable for the hens

Newcastle Disease

N ewcastle disease is a highly contagious viral infection that affects birds, including chickens. It can have devastating effects on poultry populations, leading to respiratory distress, decreased egg production, and high mortality rates. While seeking professional veterinary care is crucial, there are also natural treatments and preventive measures that can help support the health and well-being of your flock. In this blog post, we'll explore natural approaches to manage Newcastle disease and bolster the immunity of your feathered friends.

Understanding Newcastle Disease:

Newcastle disease is caused by the avian paramyxovirus, which comes in various strains. It primarily targets the respiratory, digestive, and nervous systems of birds. Recognizing the symptoms and seeking appropriate treatment is essential in managing outbreaks.

Common Signs of Newcastle Disease:

1. **Respiratory Symptoms:**

   ○ Chickens may exhibit signs such as coughing, sneezing, nasal discharge, and labored breathing.

2. **Digestive Disturbances:**

- ○ Diarrhea, loss of appetite, and reduced feed consumption may be observed.

3. **Nervous System Dysfunction (in severe cases):**

- ○ Chickens may exhibit neurological signs like trembling, circling, and paralysis.

Natural Treatments for Newcastle Disease:

1. **Echinacea:**

- ○ **Benefits:** Echinacea is known for its immune-boosting properties. It can help strengthen the immune system, aiding in recovery.

- ○ **Application:** Offer echinacea tincture in their drinking water, following dosage recommendations.

2. **Garlic and Ginger:**

- ○ **Benefits:** Both garlic and ginger have natural antiviral and immune-enhancing properties.

- ○ **Application:** Crush a clove of garlic and mix it with their food. For ginger, grate fresh ginger and add it to their feed.

3. **Herbal Infusions:**

- ○ **Benefits:** Certain herbs like oregano and thyme have natural antibacterial and antiviral properties.

- **Application:** Provide herbal infusions by steeping dried herbs in their drinking water.

4. **Honey and Lemon:**

- **Benefits:** Honey contains natural antibacterial properties, while lemon is rich in vitamin C, which supports the immune system.

- **Application:** Mix honey with warm water and offer it as a drink. Add a few drops of lemon juice to their water.

5. **Probiotics and Fermented Foods:**

- **Benefits:** Probiotics promote a healthy gut microbiome, which is crucial for overall immunity.

- **Application:** Offer yogurt, kefir, or fermented vegetables like sauerkraut in small quantities.

Preventive Measures:

1. **Biosecurity:**

- Implement strict biosecurity protocols to prevent the introduction and spread of Newcastle disease. Limit access to the coop, quarantine new birds, and disinfect equipment regularly.

2. **Vaccination:**

- In regions where Newcastle disease is prevalent, consider vaccination as a preventive measure. Consult with a veterinarian for guidance.

While natural treatments can be supportive, it's essential to consult with a veterinarian for severe cases or if symptoms persist. Combining natural remedies with good husbandry practices, such as clean living conditions and a balanced diet, will contribute to the overall health and well-being of your flock during this challenging time. With proper care and attention, you can help your chickens recover and prevent future occurrences of Newcastle disease.

OYSTER SHELLS

The Power of Oyster Shell

Oyster shell is exactly what it sounds like: crushed and ground shells from oysters, mollusks, and other shellfish. Rich in calcium carbonate, oyster shell serves as a valuable calcium supplement for chickens. Calcium is an essential nutrient that plays a crucial role in the formation of strong and healthy eggshells. Without adequate calcium, chickens may lay eggs with thinner, weaker shells, increasing the risk of breakage and other health issues.

Benefits of Using Oyster Shell for Chickens

Strong Eggshells:

A calcium-rich diet directly contributes to the formation of robust and thick eggshells. Properly calcified eggshells reduce the likelihood of breakage during laying, protecting both the eggs and the hens.

Reduced Eggshell Abnormalities:

Insufficient calcium can lead to eggshell abnormalities, including wrinkled or rough shells. Incorporating oyster shell helps minimize such irregularities.

Optimal Reproductive Health:

Calcium is vital for muscle function, including the muscles involved in egg-laying. Ensuring a consistent calcium intake supports healthy reproductive systems in hens.

Enhanced Overall Health:

Beyond eggshell strength, calcium supports bone health, blood clotting, and nerve function in chickens.

How to Offer Oyster Shell to Chickens

Separate Feeder:

Provide oyster shell in a separate feeder or container, allowing chickens to consume it as needed. Separating it from their regular feed helps them regulate their calcium intake.

Free-Choice Access:

Allow chickens free-choice access to oyster shell, ensuring they can consume it whenever they feel the need for additional calcium.

Crushed and Sifted:

Offer crushed and sifted oyster shell to ensure that the particles are of an appropriate size for easy consumption.

Monitoring Consumption:

Keep an eye on how much oyster shell your chickens consume. Adjust the amount based on their needs and laying patterns.

Supplemental Use:

Oyster shell is especially important during periods of increased egg production, such as the beginning of laying or during peak laying seasons.

Providing your chickens with oyster shell as a calcium supplement is a simple yet effective way to promote their overall health and well-being. By ensuring strong eggshells, you're not only protecting the eggs your hens produce but also supporting their reproductive health. A small addition to their diet can lead to healthier, happier chickens and a more rewarding backyard chicken-keeping experience.

parasites

C hickens can be affected by external parasites like mites, lice, and fleas, as well as internal parasites such as worms (roundworms, tapeworms, coccidia). Signs of parasitic infestation may include feather loss, weight loss, poor condition, lethargy, pale comb, and diarrhea.

Parasite control is an essential aspect of chicken health and welfare.

Here are some remedies and practices for controlling parasites in chickens:

1. **Clean and Maintain the Coop:** Regularly clean the coop and nesting boxes to minimize parasite infestation. Remove droppings, soiled bedding, and any debris where parasites can hide.

2. **Practice Deep Litter Method:** Use the deep litter method in the coop, which involves adding fresh bedding material on top of the existing litter. The beneficial microorganisms in the litter can help break down waste and reduce parasite populations.

3. **Provide Dust Bathing Areas:** Create dedicated dust bathing areas filled with sand, dirt, and diatomaceous earth (DE). Chickens instinctively use dust baths to control external parasites. DE can help suffocate and control mites and lice.

4. **Regularly Inspect Birds:** Perform routine health checks on your chickens, including close inspection of their feathers, skin, and vent area. Look for signs of external parasites like mites, lice, fleas, and ticks.

5. **Use Diatomaceous Earth (DE):** Apply food-grade diatomaceous earth to the coop and dust bathing areas. DE is a fine powder that damages the exoskeleton of insects and parasites, causing dehydration and death.

6. **Introduce Beneficial Insects:** Encourage beneficial insects like predatory mites, beetles, and nematodes in the coop and surrounding areas. They can help control populations of harmful parasites.

7. **Implement Integrated Pest Management (IPM):** Adopt an IPM approach by using a combination of strategies such

as proper sanitation, biological controls, and targeted treatments to manage parasites effectively.

8. Herbal Remedies: Some herbs have natural insect-repelling properties. Consider planting or hanging herbs like lavender, mint, rosemary, or wormwood near the coop to help deter parasites.

9. Essential Oils: Certain essential oils have insecticidal properties and can be used as natural parasite repellents. Dilute a few drops of essential oil (such as lavender, eucalyptus, or tea tree) in water and spray it around the coop, perches, and nesting areas.

10. Practice Pasture Rotation: If you allow your chickens to free-range, implement a rotational grazing system. Moving chickens to fresh pastures periodically helps break the parasite lifecycle and reduces reinfestation.

11. Regularly Clean and Treat Nesting Boxes: Clean and disinfect nesting boxes regularly to minimize the presence of mites, lice, and other parasites. Consider using natural remedies like diatomaceous earth or neem oil for treatment.

12. Maintain a Healthy Diet: A balanced diet rich in essential nutrients helps strengthen a chicken's immune system, making them more resilient to parasite infestations. Ensure chickens have access to high-quality feed appropriate for their age and breed.

13. **Use Commercial Products:** There are various commercially available natural or organic pest control products specifically formulated for poultry. Follow the instructions provided by the manufacturer and use them as directed.

14. **Practice Fecal Egg Counts:** Periodically collect fecal samples from your chickens and conduct fecal egg counts to monitor internal parasite levels. This can help determine if deworming is necessary and inform treatment decisions.

15. **Deworming:** Consult with a veterinarian to develop a deworming schedule appropriate for your flock. Deworming medications should be used judiciously and rotated to prevent parasite resistance.

Remember, prevention is key when it comes to parasite control. Good husbandry practices, regular monitoring, and maintaining a clean and healthy environment are crucial for minimizing parasite infestations in chickens. It's always recommended to consult with a poultry veterinarian for specific advice and guidance based on your flock's needs and local conditions.

PaSTY BUTT

P asty butt, also known as pasting, is a common condition in chicks where droppings stick to the down feathers around their vent area, blocking their ability to defecate properly. If left unattended, it can lead to serious health issues. Here's how to clean pasty butt in chicks:

1. Prepare the necessary supplies: **Before you start, gather the following supplies:**
• Warm water (not hot)
• Mild dish soap or poultry-safe shampoo
• Soft cloth or cotton balls
• Towel
• Hairdryer (optional, set on low and at a safe distance)

2. **Inspect the chick:** Carefully examine the chick's vent area to determine the severity of the pasting. If the droppings are

hardened or tightly stuck, you may need to soften them before attempting to remove them.

3. **Soak and loosen the droppings:** Gently wet a soft cloth or cotton ball with warm water and apply it to the affected area around the vent. Allow the warm water to soak the droppings and soften them. Be patient and give the water enough time to work.

4. **Gently remove the droppings:** Once the droppings have softened, use the soft cloth or cotton ball to gently wipe away the droppings from the chick's down feathers. Be careful not to pull on the feathers or cause any discomfort to the chick. Take your time and work slowly.

5. **Clean the vent area:** After removing the droppings, dampen a clean cloth or cotton ball with warm water and a small amount of mild dish soap or poultry-safe shampoo. Gently clean the vent area to ensure it is thoroughly cleaned and free from any residue.

6. **Dry the chick:** Use a towel to carefully pat the chick dry. If the chick is cold or damp, you can use a hairdryer on low and at a safe distance to help dry the chick, but be cautious not to expose the chick to direct heat or hold the hairdryer too close.

7. **Monitor and repeat if necessary:** Keep a close eye on the chick to ensure that pasty butt does not reoccur. If needed,

repeat the cleaning process as necessary to prevent the buildup of droppings.

8. **Check the chick's overall health:** Pasty butt can be a sign of underlying health issues or stress in chicks. Monitor the chick's overall well-being, ensure they are eating and drinking properly, and provide a clean and warm environment.

It's important to address pasty butt promptly to prevent discomfort, infection, and potential health complications in chicks. If the condition persists or worsens despite your efforts, or if the chick appears sick, it's advisable to seek veterinary advice for further evaluation and treatment.

Permethrin-Based Products

P ermethrin-based products are commonly used to control and treat mite infestations in chickens. Permethrin is a synthetic insecticide that is effective against a wide range of pests, including mites. Here are some key points about permethrin-based products for mite control in chickens:

1. **Formulations:** Permethrin is available in various formulations, including sprays, powders, dusts, and concentrated solutions. These products are designed to be applied directly to the birds or used to treat the coop and surrounding areas.

2. **Application:** Follow the instructions provided on the product label for proper application. This may involve spraying or dusting the birds, their feathers, and the areas

where mites are likely to hide, such as cracks, crevices, and bedding material.

3. **Safety Considerations:** When using permethrin-based products, it's important to follow safety precautions and use them as directed. Wear protective gloves, clothing, and eyewear when applying the product, and avoid direct contact with your skin. Keep the product away from children and pets. If using a spray, ensure proper ventilation in the area to prevent inhalation.

4. **Reapplication:** Depending on the severity of the mite infestation, you may need to reapply the permethrin-based product as recommended by the manufacturer. Mite eggs can be resistant to treatment, so repeat applications may be necessary to target newly hatched mites.

5. **Withdrawal Period:** If you're using permethrin-based products on chickens raised for meat or eggs, make sure to check the product label for any specified withdrawal period. This is the period of time required between the last application and when the meat or eggs can be consumed to ensure no residues remain.

6. **Integrated Pest Management (IPM):** While permethrin-based products can be effective, it's often recommended to incorporate other strategies as part of an integrated pest management approach. This may include regular coop cleaning, proper ventilation, use of natural remedies, and maintaining good overall flock health.

It's essential to carefully read and follow the instructions provided with the specific permethrin-based product you choose, as formulations and application guidelines may vary. Additionally, if you have any concerns or questions, consult with a veterinarian or poultry health professional for guidance on the appropriate use of permethrin-based products for mite control in chickens.

Probiotics

1. Probiotics help maintain a healthy gut flora, improve digestion, and boost the immune system of chickens. You can provide probiotic supplements specifically formulated for poultry or offer fermented foods like yogurt or kefir.

Probiotics are live microorganisms that are beneficial for our health, particularly for our digestive system. They are often referred to as "good bacteria" and can provide various health benefits.

Here are some key points about probiotics:

1. **Types of Probiotics:** Probiotics can include different strains of bacteria or yeasts. Some common types of probiotics include Lactobacillus and Bifidobacterium

species. Each strain may have specific benefits and target different areas of the digestive tract.

2. Gut Health: Probiotics play a crucial role in maintaining a healthy balance of bacteria in the gut. They can help promote digestion, nutrient absorption, and a healthy immune system. They also assist in preventing the overgrowth of harmful bacteria in the gut.

3. **Digestive Health Benefits:** Probiotics have been associated with various digestive health benefits, such as alleviating symptoms of diarrhea, irritable bowel syndrome (IBS), and inflammatory bowel disease (IBD). They may also help improve digestion and relieve constipation.

4. **Immune System Support:** The gut is closely linked to the immune system, and probiotics can support immune function. They help regulate the immune response and enhance the production of antibodies, potentially reducing the risk of certain infections and allergies.

5. **Antibiotic-Associated Diarrhea:** Probiotics can be beneficial for individuals taking antibiotics, as they can help prevent or reduce antibiotic-associated diarrhea. Antibiotics can disrupt the natural balance of gut bacteria, and probiotics can help restore it.

6. **Sources of Probiotics:** Probiotics can be found in certain foods and supplements. Fermented foods like yogurt, kefir, sauerkraut, kimchi, and kombucha often contain live and

active cultures of beneficial bacteria. Probiotic supplements
are also available, providing specific strains in concentrated
forms.

7. **Choosing Probiotic Supplements:** When selecting a
probiotic supplement, consider factors such as the specific
strains included, the number of live organisms (colony-forming units,
or CFUs), and any additional ingredients.
Different strains may have different effects, so it's important
to choose a probiotic that suits your specific needs

Remedies to Promote Health

1. Provide a balanced diet with appropriate nutrition.

2. Ensure access to clean, fresh water at all times.

3. Offer a variety of herbs, such as oregano, thyme, and garlic, which can support immune health.

4. Use apple cider vinegar (ACV) as a natural supplement in the water to promote digestive health.

5. Incorporate probiotics to support gut health.

6. Avoid overcrowding in the coop to reduce stress and prevent disease spread.

7. Provide ample space for exercise and foraging.

8. Create dust bathing areas to help control mites and parasites.

9. Plant chicken-friendly herbs like mint, basil, and parsley, which can provide additional nutrients and natural insect repellents.

10. Use diatomaceous earth as a natural remedy for external parasites.

11. Provide access to sunlight for vitamin D synthesis.

12. Offer a well-ventilated coop to prevent respiratory issues.

13. Maintain a clean coop and regularly remove droppings to minimize bacteria and odor.

14. Provide a secure coop and run to protect chickens from predators.

15. Use natural nesting materials, such as straw or dried herbs, for comfortable nesting boxes.

16. Avoid using toxic cleaning products in the coop.

17. Plant chicken-safe flowers, such as marigolds and calendula, which can help repel pests.

18. Create shaded areas in the run to protect chickens from extreme heat.

19. Offer occasional treats like fruits, vegetables, and mealworms in moderation.

20. Hang bundles of herbs, like lavender or chamomile, to provide natural stress relief.

21. Use essential oils, such as eucalyptus or lavender, sparingly and safely for pest control or coop deodorizing.

22. Provide natural sources of calcium, such as crushed eggshells or oyster shell, for strong eggshells.

23. Use pine shavings or straw as bedding material.

24. Avoid using cedar shavings as they can be toxic to chickens.

25. Keep the coop dry to prevent fungal and bacterial infections.

26. Ensure proper ventilation to minimize ammonia buildup.

27. Quarantine new chickens before introducing them to the flock to prevent disease spread.

28. Offer occasional treats of fermented feed, which can improve digestion.

29. Trim overgrown beaks, nails, and spurs as needed.

30. Introduce natural deterrents, like predator decoys or motion-activated sprinklers, to deter predators.

31. Rotate grazing areas to prevent parasite buildup.

32. Provide perches of varying heights to promote exercise and prevent foot issues.

33. Keep food and water containers clean to avoid bacterial contamination.

34. Avoid using chemical-based pesticides or herbicides in areas accessible to chickens.

35. Provide access to shade and shelter during inclement weather.

36. Keep a close eye on chicken behavior to identify any signs of illness or stress.

37. Plant beneficial trees or shrubs to provide shade, shelter, and natural forage.

38. Avoid using treated wood or toxic materials in the coop or run.

39. Integrate beneficial insects like ladybugs or praying mantises to control pests naturally.

40. Use natural fly repellents, like fly traps or herbs such as lavender or mint.

41. Regularly trim and maintain the chicken's feathers for cleanliness and comfort.

42. Encourage natural foraging by allowing chickens to free-range when safe and appropriate.

43. Create separate areas for sick or injured chickens to recover.

44. Incorporate garlic into the diet as a natural dewormer.

45. Provide access to grit for proper digestion.

46. Use natural predators, such as beneficial nematodes, to control harmful pests.

47. Maintain a consistent daily routine for feeding and care.

48. Use natural solutions, like neem oil or herbal sprays, for external parasite control.

49. Offer natural sources of entertainment, such as hanging cabbage or corn cobs, to reduce boredom.

50. Consult with an experienced poultry veterinarian for guidance on natural remedies and care practices specific to your region.

Remember, while natural remedies can be beneficial, it's important to consult a veterinarian for specific advice and guidance tailored to your chickens' health and well-being.

Respiratory Infections

R espiratory infections, such as infectious bronchitis,
infectious laryngotracheitis, and mycoplasma gallisepticum,
can cause symptoms like coughing, sneezing, nasal
discharge, difficulty breathing, and decreased egg
production

salmonellosis

S almonellosis is a bacterial infection caused by the pathogenic strains of Salmonella. This disease poses a significant threat to poultry health, potentially leading to symptoms like diarrhea, lethargy, decreased appetite, and, in severe cases, fatalities. Recognizing the causes and implementing natural remedies is essential in managing this ailment and safeguarding the well-being of your flock. In this chapter, we'll delve into the intricacies of salmonellosis, from its origins to effective natural treatment options.

Understanding Salmonellosis:

Salmonellosis is caused by various strains of Salmonella bacteria, which can be found in contaminated food, water, and environments. In chickens, it primarily affects the digestive system, leading to a range of clinical signs.

Common Signs of Salmonellosis:

1. **Diarrhea:** Chickens affected by salmonellosis may experience watery or bloody diarrhea.

2. **Lethargy and Weakness:** Infected chickens often display

signs of lethargy, weakness, and a lack of energy.

3. **Reduced Appetite:** Chickens may lose interest in food, leading to decreased feed consumption.

4. **Weight Loss:** Prolonged illness can result in noticeable weight loss.

5. **Dehydration:** Severe cases of salmonellosis can lead to dehydration, further exacerbating the condition.

Causes of Salmonellosis:

1. **Contaminated Environment:**

   ○ **Explanation:** Bacteria can thrive in environments where hygiene and sanitation are lacking. Contaminated bedding, water, and feed can introduce Salmonella to the flock.

2. **Carrier Birds:**

   ○ **Explanation:** Chickens can carry Salmonella without displaying symptoms, acting as reservoirs and potentially spreading the infection to others.

3. **Contaminated Feed and Water:**

   ○ **Explanation:** Moldy or contaminated feed and water sources can introduce Salmonella to the digestive system.

Natural Remedies for Salmonellosis:

1. **Probiotics:**

   ○ **Benefits:** Probiotics help restore healthy gut bacteria and support the immune system's response to infection.

- **Application:** Administer probiotics via water or feed according to recommended dosage.

2. Apple Cider Vinegar:

- **Benefits:** Apple cider vinegar has natural antibacterial properties and can help create an inhospitable environment for pathogens in the digestive tract.

- **Application:** Add a small amount to their drinking water.

3. Ginger and Turmeric:

- **Benefits:** Both ginger and turmeric possess anti-inflammatory and immune-boosting properties.

- **Application:** Incorporate fresh or dried ginger and turmeric into their feed.

4. Garlic:

- **Benefits:** Garlic is known for its natural antibacterial properties and can support the immune system.

- **Application:** Crush a clove of garlic and mix it with their food.

5. Chamomile Infusions:

- **Benefits:** Chamomile has anti-inflammatory properties and can help soothe the digestive system.

○ **Application:** Provide chamomile-infused water as a drink.

Salmonellosis is a serious bacterial infection that requires prompt attention. While natural remedies can be supportive, it's crucial to consult with a veterinarian for severe cases or if symptoms persist. Combining natural remedies with strict biosecurity measures and a balanced diet will contribute to the overall health and well-being of your flock during this challenging time. With proper care and attention, you can help your chickens recover and prevent future occurrences of salmonellosis.

SOFT-SHELLED EGG

A soft-shelled egg, also known as a "rubbery egg" or "shell-less egg," is a condition where a chicken lays an egg with a thin or incomplete shell. This can be a common occurrence, but it's essential to address the issue to ensure the health and well-being of your flock. Here are the causes and remedies for soft-shelled eggs:

Causes:

Calcium Deficiency:

Cause: Insufficient calcium in the diet is one of the primary reasons for soft-shelled eggs. Calcium is essential for strong eggshell formation.

Remedy: Ensure that your hens have access to a balanced diet with a sufficient supply of calcium. This can be provided through commercial layer feeds or supplements like crushed oyster shells.

Stress:

Cause: High-stress levels in chickens, caused by factors like overcrowding, predator threats, or changes in the environment, can disrupt the egg-laying process and lead to soft shells.

Remedy: Provide a calm and secure environment for your flock. Minimize potential stressors and ensure that your chickens have ample space and a comfortable coop.

Age of the Hen:

Cause: Young hens that have recently started laying or older hens nearing the end of their laying cycle may experience irregularities in eggshell formation, including soft shells.

Remedy: While age-related changes are natural, maintaining a balanced diet with adequate calcium and other nutrients can help mitigate soft shell occurrences.

Vitamin D Deficiency:

Cause: Vitamin D is crucial for calcium absorption. Chickens with insufficient exposure to natural sunlight or those lacking vitamin D in their diet may produce eggs with weak or soft shells.

Remedy: Ensure that your flock receives regular exposure to sunlight or provide them with a balanced diet that includes vitamin D-rich foods or supplements.

Genetic Factors:

Cause: Some chicken breeds are more prone to producing soft-shelled eggs due to genetic predispositions.

Remedy: While genetic factors can't be changed, providing a well-balanced diet with sufficient calcium can help mitigate soft-shell occurrences.

Additional Tips:

Monitor Egg Production: Keep track of how often soft-shelled eggs occur. If it's a persistent issue, consider consulting a veterinarian to rule out any underlying health concerns.

Provide Clean Water: Ensure your chickens have access to clean, fresh water at all times. Dehydration can affect eggshell quality.

Maintain a Clean Coop: A clean environment reduces the likelihood of bacterial contamination, which can contribute to soft shells.

Gradual Diet Changes: If you're transitioning to a new feed or making dietary adjustments, do so gradually to allow your chickens' digestive systems to adapt.

Consult a Veterinarian: If the issue persists despite implementing remedies, seek advice from a veterinarian who specializes in poultry health.

By addressing the underlying causes and implementing appropriate remedies, you can help your flock produce eggs with strong, healthy shells, ensuring the well-being of your chickens and the quality of the eggs they lay.

sour crop

S our crop, also known as crop stasis or impacted crop, is a condition where the crop—the pouch-like organ at the base of a chicken's neck—becomes distended, sour-smelling, and impacted due to an imbalance of microorganisms in the digestive tract. This condition can lead to discomfort, poor digestion, and potentially more severe health issues if left untreated.

Diagnosing Sour Crop

Crop Examination:

Begin by gently feeling the crop in the morning before feeding. A healthy crop should feel relatively empty or like a water balloon. A sour crop may feel doughy, swollen, or squishy.

Sour Odor:

When a chicken has sour crop, the crop may emit a foul smell, resembling a vinegar-like odor.

Behavioral Changes:

Chickens with sour crop may exhibit signs of discomfort, such as lethargy, decreased appetite, or reluctance to move.

Vomiting or Regurgitation:

Observe if the chicken regurgitates or vomits liquid or partially digested food. This is a telltale sign of sour crop.

Changes in Crop Shape:

An abnormally shaped or unevenly distended crop could indicate an underlying issue.

Treatment of Sour Crop

Empty the Crop:

If the crop is impacted, gently empty its contents by carefully massaging it. Ensure the chicken's head is lower than its body to prevent aspiration.

Flush the Crop:

Offer electrolyte solution (without sugar) to the chicken to help flush the crop and rehydrate them.

Probiotics:

Introduce probiotics or plain yogurt to promote the growth of beneficial bacteria in the digestive tract.

Limit Food Intake:

Temporarily limit food intake to soft, easily digestible foods like cooked rice or oatmeal. This gives the crop time to recover.

Elevate Roosts:

Elevate roosts to discourage chickens from roosting overnight, which can contribute to the development of sour crop.

Apple Cider Vinegar:

Some chicken keepers use diluted apple cider vinegar in water as a preventive measure to maintain a healthy crop balance.

When to Seek Veterinary Help

While mild cases of sour crop can be managed at home, severe cases or those that do not improve within a few days require veterinary attention. A veterinarian can provide professional guidance, perform necessary procedures, and prescribe medications if needed.

Sour crop is a distressing condition that can affect the well-being of your chickens. By familiarizing yourself with its symptoms, promptly diagnosing the issue, and implementing appropriate treatment strategies, you can ensure the health and happiness of your feathered flock. Remember, a watchful eye, proactive care, and regular health checks are crucial in maintaining a thriving and joyful chicken-keeping experience.

THRUSH

C hicken thrush is caused by the Candida albicans fungus, which naturally resides in a chicken's digestive tract. When there's an imbalance in the gut's microorganisms or the immune system is compromised, this fungus can overgrow and lead to infection.

Diagnosing Chicken Thrush

Oral Lesions:

Inspect your chickens' mouths for white, cheesy patches on the tongue, roof of the mouth, or throat. These lesions are a common sign of thrush.

Reduced Appetite and Weight Loss:

Chickens with thrush may show a decreased interest in food and subsequently lose weight.

Difficulty Swallowing:

Observe if your chickens exhibit difficulty swallowing or regurgitate their food.

Discolored Droppings:

Abnormal, discolored droppings that appear greenish or grayish can be indicative of a digestive issue like thrush.

Lethargy and Weakness:

Chickens affected by thrush may become lethargic, weak, and less active than usual.

Treating Chicken Thrush

Antifungal Treatment:

Consult a veterinarian for antifungal medications or treatments. These can come in the form of medicated water, feed additives, or oral gels.

Isolate Infected Birds:

Isolate infected chickens to prevent the spread of the fungus to healthy birds.

Supportive Care:

Provide easily digestible, nutritious food, and ensure access to clean water. A balanced diet can boost the immune system's ability to fight off infections.

Hygiene and Cleanliness:

Maintain a clean coop environment, including regular cleaning of feeders and waterers, to minimize the risk of fungal overgrowth.

Probiotics:

Introduce probiotics to promote a healthy gut environment and restore the balance of beneficial microorganisms.

Boost Immunity:

Enhance your chickens' immunity with stress reduction, proper nutrition, and a well-ventilated, dry living space.

Preventing Chicken Thrush

Balanced Diet:

Provide a balanced and nutritious diet to support optimal gut health.

Hygiene Practices:

Keep feeders, waterers, and the coop clean and dry to prevent fungal growth.

Stress Reduction:

Minimize stressors like overcrowding, sudden changes, and extreme weather conditions.

Caring for your chickens means being proactive about their health. By recognizing the symptoms, promptly diagnosing, and effectively treating chicken thrush, you're ensuring the well-being and happiness of your flock. Regular health checks, hygienic practices, and a balanced diet play pivotal roles in preventing fungal infections like thrush. Remember, a vigilant eye and responsible care make for a healthier and more joyful chicken-keeping experience.

VENT CLEANING

A chicken's vent, also known as the cloaca, is the external opening at the rear end of a chicken's body. It is the common opening for the intestinal, urinary, and reproductive systems. The vent is where a chicken expels waste, including feces and urine, as well as where eggs are laid.

The vent is a small, puckered opening located just below the chicken's tail feathers. It is covered by a flap of skin known as the vent orifice, which can open and close. The vent is a sensitive area and should be handled with care.

It's important to keep the vent area clean and free from soiling to maintain the chicken's overall health and prevent potential issues such as infections or blockages. Regular cleaning of the coop, nesting boxes, and perches can help minimize the risk of contamination in the vent area.

Additionally, ensuring the chickens have a well-balanced diet, access to clean water, and appropriate flock management practices can contribute to maintaining a healthy vent.

VENT CLEANING

Cleaning a chicken's vent is a delicate process that may be necessary if the area becomes soiled or blocked. It's important to approach this task with care to avoid causing any harm to the chicken. Here's a step-by-step guide on how to clean a chicken's vent:

1. Prepare the necessary supplies: Before you start, gather the following supplies:
• Warm water (not hot)
• Mild dish soap or poultry-safe shampoo
• Soft cloth or cotton balls
• Towel
• Gloves (optional)

2. Secure the chicken: Ensure the chicken is calm and secure to minimize stress. You may need someone to assist you in safely restraining the chicken, especially if it tends to be skittish.

3. Assess the situation: Carefully examine the chicken's vent area to determine the severity of the soiling or

blockage. If the vent is excessively dirty or if there is a blockage, you may need to proceed with cleaning.

4. Wet the area: Dampen a soft cloth or cotton ball with warm water and gently apply it to the vent area. Allow the warm water to soak and soften any dried or stuck-on matter.

5. Clean the vent: With a gentle touch, use the soft cloth or cotton ball to clean around the vent area. You can add a small amount of mild dish soap or poultry-safe shampoo to the cloth or directly to the area to assist in removing any stubborn dirt or residue. Be cautious and avoid inserting anything into the vent itself.

6. Rinse the area: Use a clean cloth or cotton ball dampened with warm water to rinse the vent area. Ensure that all soap or shampoo is thoroughly removed. Be gentle to avoid causing any discomfort to the chicken.

7. Dry the chicken: Use a towel to carefully pat the chicken dry, especially in the vent area. Ensure the chicken is adequately dried to prevent chilling.

8. Observe the chicken: After cleaning, keep an eye on the chicken to ensure that the vent remains clean and unobstructed. If there are any signs of continued blockage, inflammation, or other concerning symptoms, consult a veterinarian for further evaluation.

It's crucial to maintain a clean and hygienic environment for your chickens to help prevent issues like soiling or blockage of the vent. Regularly cleaning the coop, nesting boxes, and perches can help minimize the likelihood of the vent area becoming soiled.

Additionally, ensuring the chickens have access to a balanced diet, clean water, and appropriate flock management practices can contribute to overall vent health. If you have concerns or encounter persistent issues with a chicken's vent, it's always advisable to seek veterinary advice for proper diagnosis and guidance

WHITE EGG YOLKS

When you crack open an egg, you probably expect to find a bright, yellow yolk. After all, that's the classic image we have of eggs. However, you may be surprised to learn that not all egg yolks are yellow; some can be white. This curious phenomenon has intrigued many egg enthusiasts and culinary experts alike. In this blog post, we'll delve into the reasons behind why some egg yolks are white and what it means for the quality and nutritional value of the egg.

Diet of the Hen

The primary factor influencing the color of an egg yolk is the diet of the laying hen. Hens that are fed a diet low in pigments, such as carotenoids, which are responsible for the yellow and orange hues in yolks, will produce eggs with paler yolks. On the other hand, hens that have access to a diet rich in carotenoids, like those found in yellow corn, marigold petals, or alfalfa, will lay eggs with vibrant, yellow yolks.

Breed of the Hen

Different chicken breeds can produce eggs with varying yolk colors. Some breeds naturally lay eggs with pale yolks, while others produce eggs with rich, golden yolks. For example, breeds like Leghorns are known for their white eggs with lighter yolks, while Rhode Island Reds are known for their brown eggs with darker yolks.

Age of the Hen

As hens age, the color of their yolks can change. Younger hens tend to produce eggs with lighter yolks, while older hens may lay eggs with darker yolks. This is not a drastic change but can be observed over time.

Stress Levels and Health of the Hen

Stress and poor health can also impact the color of egg yolks. Hens that are stressed or suffering from health issues may produce eggs with paler yolks. Ensuring that your hens are well-cared-for and in good health is essential for consistent egg quality.

Genetics

Genetics play a role in the color of egg yolks. Some chicken breeds are genetically predisposed to lay eggs with specific yolk colors. These genetic factors interact with the hen's diet to determine the final color of the yolk.

Nutritional Value and Taste

The color of the yolk does not necessarily reflect its nutritional value. Both white and yellow yolks are nutritious, containing essential vitamins, minerals, and proteins. The taste of the yolk is also not significantly affected by its color; it primarily depends on the hen's diet and overall health.

The color of an egg yolk, whether white or yellow, is a result of various factors, including the hen's diet, breed, age, stress levels, and genetics. While it's true that yolks can come in a range of colors, it's important to note that the color has no bearing on the egg's nutritional value or taste. So, whether you prefer your yolks sunny yellow or pale white, rest assured that the eggs you choose are a nutritious and delicious choice for your culinary endeavors.

community invitation

At Natural Remedies for Backyard Chickens Blog, we've created a space where like-minded individuals come together to share insights, exchange ideas, and support one another on the journey to happy, healthy hens. Whether you're a seasoned chicken keeper or just starting out, our community offers a wealth of resources, tips, and experiences to enrich your chicken-raising adventure.

Here's a glimpse of what you can expect as a member:

1. **Engaging Discussions:** Participate in lively conversations with fellow chicken enthusiasts, sharing your experiences, asking questions, and offering valuable advice.

2. **Exclusive Content:** Gain access to members-only articles, guides, and resources on natural remedies, coop management, and all things chickens!

3. **Expert Insights:** Interact with experienced chicken keepers and experts who regularly contribute their knowledge and insights to the community.

4. **Inspiring Stories:** Read heartwarming tales of successful chicken-raising journeys and share your own to inspire and encourage others.

5. **Monthly Challenges:** Take part in fun and educational challenges designed to enhance your skills and deepen your understanding of caring for backyard chickens naturally.

Joining our online community is easy! Simply visit Natural Remedies for Backyard Chickens Blog and click on the "Join Community" button to get started.

We can't wait to welcome you into our flock of passionate backyard chicken enthusiasts. Together, we'll create a supportive and informative space where our shared love for these feathery friends can thrive.

Here's to healthy, happy chickens and a vibrant online community!

Made in United States
Troutdale, OR
10/11/2023

13601497R00096